DIARY OF A TRAIN-SPOTTER

Volume 1
1955-59

Nostalgic recollections of visits to locomotive depots, workshops, railway stations and scrapyards

Michael G. Harvey

Silver Link Publishing Ltd

This book is dedicated to the memory of my good friend David Copus, who tragically died at the age of 48 shortly before publication. Apart from contributing to the photographic material used in the book, David was a regular companion on many of my trips. In the days of steam, his home, a mere 100 yards from Fratton Locomotive Depot entrance, was a regular meeting-place for fellow enthusiasts. More recently David kept in touch with the preservation scene with regular visits to the 'Watercress Line' and locations in South Wales where his sister now lives.

The author (centre) with his close friends Eddie Rooke (left) and David Copus. Without their help this book would not have been possible.

ACKNOWLEDGEMENTS

In appreciation of the assistance received in compiling this book, my sincere thanks must firstly go to my close friends Eddie Rooke and David Copus, both of Portsmouth. I list below, in alphabetical order, other persons who have in some way or other contributed information to help bring this book together. If I have missed anyone out, please accept my apologies.

Colin Asprey, Eastleigh; Basil Batten, Cosham; David Bird, Eastney; Alan Crockford, Fareham; A. D. Davies, Portchester; Ron Davies, Cosham; Peter Esgate, Portsmouth; Gerald A. Jacobs, Woking; G. E. 'Jim' Jackson, Pentraeth, Gwynedd; Ron Jelley, Abertillery; Bill Jenkins, Gosport; John Kinchen, Bedhampton; Jim Lawrence, Portsmouth; George Pearce, Cardiff; the late R. Ricketts, Portsmouth; M. H. Rowe, Nottingham; A. Sheppard, Isle of Wight; Bob Smith, Bedhampton; Jack Stillwell, Portsmouth; Andrew Sutherland, Cosham; J. H. Websper, Margate; Bob Whitney, Portsmouth; R. Yates, Ramsgate; Mike Yerbury, Southsea.

Special thanks are also due to (in alphabetical order): Ian Allan Publishing Ltd; British Railways Board; Carreras Limited; Hull Museum of Transport; Isle of Wight Steam Railway; Kellogg Co of Great Britain Limited; The National Tramway Museum, Crich; *The News*, Portsmouth (formerly *The Evening News*); Portsmouth Football Company Limited; Reynards Cards of Bath; Swindon Railway Museum.

Also, again in alphabetical order, some of the names and nicknames of railway enthusiasts with whom I associated during the years 1955 to 1968, who have not all necessarily been referred to in this book: Frank Allen; Tony Alton; Michael Ashcroft; Don Aylward; Charlie Best; 'Gaffer' Bleach; David Bodenham; 'Cardiff'; Vic Coppin; Mike Chapman; Mike Dooley; 'Gasser', Ian Gray; David Greenfield; Terry Hunt; Tony Ingram; John 'Plymouth' Jones; Timothy Julnes; Jack Knowler; 'Norman'; Trevor 'Haggis' Robson; Roger Wade; Doug Willis; Roy Wiltshire; and Dave Woolley.

In addition, I would like to say 'thank you' to my wife Ann for her help in the early days in compiling copy and in the latter years for being very patient in putting up with masses of paper, photographs and a very trusty Olivetti 22 typewriter which had found a permanent place on the lounge dining-table. She knew that one day 'the book' would be completed and the lounge table would once again return to normal.

Finally, thanks to Eddie Rooke for his assistance and knowledge in helping to condense the original 800 pages to fit this book and the subsequent volumes.

CONTENTS

First published in April 1993

British Library Cataloguing in Publication Data

Harvey, Michael G.
    Diary of a Train-spotter: Nostalgic Recollections of
    Visits to Locomotive Depots, Workshops, Railway
    Stations and Scrapyards, 1955-68
    I. Title
    385.092

ISBN 1 85794 004 0

Silver Link Publishing Ltd
Unit 5
Home Farm Close
Church Street
Wadenhoe
Peterborough PE8 5TE
Tel/fax (08015) 4-4-0

Printed and bound in Great Britain

Remember that deliberate fare evasion is an offence, and that trespassing on the railway is both illegal and dangerous.

PREFACE

When I left Kingston Secondary Modern School for Boys in Portsmouth in the summer of 1956, I had previously taken an examination for a joiner's job in Portsmouth Naval Dockyard, but unfortunately, after passing the exam, this particular job was not available to me. It was then that I decided that my interest in railways, which had been steadily growing for over a year, would be best utilised if I could get a job on British Railways. All teenaged boys wanted to be a train driver, and I suppose that I was no exception, so off I went one sunny December morning in 1956, walking along Goldsmith Avenue, past the Southern Region electric units' large depot, to the entrance gate of Fratton Locomotive Depot.

On my arrival I met the Shed Foreman, a Mr Butler, to whom I explained that I was very keen to learn the job of a train driver. He told me briefly that if I passed a medical and was physically fit, I would begin as a cleaner and then work my way up through the grades to become a fireman and eventually driver, this, he stressed, sometimes taking up to 15 years to achieve.

A little while later I made the short rail journey to Eastleigh where I entered a very large building in the Locomotive Works yard and underwent a very thorough medical examination. I well remember the doctor displaying, very quickly, coloured discs which had similarly coloured numerals engraved in them, and asking me to identify each numeral as it flashed in front of my eyes. Of course good vision is an essential part of a job of this nature and it

was here that I failed - my right eye was perfect, but the left one not so. A few days later I received a letter telling me this. I was quite upset and dejected and began blaming my earlier school days and the local health authorities for not issuing me with spectacles; over a number of years one magnified glass in the left side could have made all the difference.

Nevertheless, what had or had not been done in the past was too late now. I could have easily got employment as a railway porter, but I did not want that - perhaps I should have looked into various other jobs on the railway, such as signalling, permanent way maintenance or painting in the Works yard at Eastleigh. But the dream of becoming a train driver had now been shattered and I resigned myself to finding another job.

This I did, with a firm in the printing industry, Grosvenor Press. A close friend of mine, David Wills, who had left the same school before me, became a compositor and one day he visited me to show me a proof of several paragraphs of hand-set type. He explained briefly to me about the job and the reader's marks on the proof; I became interested and several weeks later I took an aptitude test and passed with a 75 per cent mark. I thus started work on Monday 7 January 1957 as an apprentice compositor; this apprenticeship, after and including a three-month trial period, lasted for six years.

I do not claim to be an author or a photographer, but I do hope to convey to you through this book my simple, straightforward lists of locomotive numbers, references

and highlights, together with all my other personal exploits and experiences that occurred whenever a railway trip was made.

The least said about the camera with which I took many of the photographs the better! It was a proud possession of my late father - a Brownie Box camera dating back to 1926, which when new would

have cost between 17/6d and 27/6d. It used a 120 film. I had no experience of using a camera prior to 1957, and this shows in many of the pictures in my original 800-page book which regrettably were not of a quality fit for publishing. Many pictures were taken 'on the spur of the moment' - sometimes with the engine's chimney or even its driving wheels cut short in the photograph! The one thing that I am proud of is that I actually took photographs of steam locomotives as far back as 1957, whereas many of my friends at Fratton never took any pictures. I kept all my negatives stored away in an old biscuit tin, and some had never been touched for well over 15 years, some nearer 20 years, until I brought them 'to light' for the book.

Diary of a Train-spotter is a railway journey lasting 14 years and describes the adventures that I and many of my friends who accompanied me became involved in. It was basically train-spotting, but much more interesting. We sometimes broke the rules by entering depots without permits, but never did any of us at any time resort to causing violence or damage. Looking back, I cannot recall any enthusiasts mentioned in this book who were wary or had second thoughts about travelling to any strange city or town, day or night, including London, for the first time - there was an air of adventure in *every* trip, whether it was local or distant. Sadly, in my opinion this adventure has now gone and modern train-spotters have been left to jot down the numbers of 'boxes on wheels' and breathe in diesel fumes, in an age where the venue of your trip is decided by the society that it houses.

Muggings, etc, are now an everyday hazard - a far cry from those days of the 1950s and 1960s when one could travel by rail anywhere, day or night, in comfort and without the fears that today's modern enthusiasts have to be constantly aware of.

INTRODUCTION

It was perhaps some time in 1950, at the age of nine and when I was living at Fifth Street, Fratton, that I first began to take notice of railway engines. Although I can recollect going to see them on many occasions, it was not until 1955, by which time I had moved house the short distance to Penhale Road, that I began collecting numbers in earnest. At Penhale Road I was ideally situated in that I was barely 5 minutes' walk away from Fratton station and only 2 minutes away from 'Sooty Footbridge' which was one of the railway workers' entrances to the locomotive depot.

At Fratton station the footbridge spans all the railway lines into Portsmouth, covering an area between the station forecourt and Goldsmith Avenue, and was the focal meeting-place of many railway enthusiasts, both young and old. I spent many happy hours train-spotting from this vantage point, which in those days had windows on both sides and a completely covered roof. I don't think that I can ever recall seeing the windows completely clear of soot and dirt, especially those directly above the railway tracks serving platforms 1, 2 and 3 - even so, we always managed to see through the grime just enough to note the engine numbers.

The other meeting-place, not as popular as Fratton station footbridge, was 'Sooty Footbridge', which was accessible via a private side entrance in Walmer Road, and linked the terraced-house Fratton area directly with the depot yard. Enthusiasts very rarely used this bridge to gain entrance to the depot as one could easily be spotted by railwaymen and signalling staff at the now demolished Fratton East signal box; it was regarded as a 'railway workers only' bridge, and was dismantled during the mid or late 1950s.

Meeting other railway enthusiasts on Fratton station footbridge was commonplace and we always compared notes and asked what classes of locomotives had either gone down to the 'Town' (Portsmouth & Southsea) or if any notable locomotive had gone 'on shed'. Portsmouth Town station had in fact been re-named Portsmouth & Southsea as long ago as 1921, but the old name always seemed to stick with our parents and the elderly people in the city. Even in the late 1960s and, to a lesser extent, today, people still refer to Portsmouth & Southsea as the 'Town' station - old memories die hard.

The depot yard and the roundhouse were clearly visible from the station footbridge, and one could identify a handful of different classes although their numbers were too far away to identify without the use of binoculars.

Some of the younger train-spotters that gathered on the footbridge were only ever known to me by their nicknames, but nevertheless we did converse on all the local railway gossip in and around Fratton. It was in these very early days that I met my future railway friends, Eddie Rooke, David Copus, Frank Allen, Jim Lawrence, Terry Hunt, Tony Ingram, Bill Jenkins, Dave Bodenham and many others far too numerous to mention.

Eddie Rooke, who lived at Sandringham Road, Fratton, was a very keen railway enthusiast and together we gradually got round to making plans to travel to and visit other stations and depots within not too great a distance of Portsmouth. Looking back, I can see that our interest in railways, and Southern Region steam in particular, all began on that foot-bridge at Fratton station, together with the occasional visit to the depot, and I recall all the many good times that I and other enthusiasts always enjoyed whenever we met. Many a time my mother, after shopping in Fratton Road, would turn up at the station foot-bridge to remind me that my dinner had been in the oven for several hours! Endless hours were spent at this location, especially in the summer months when the local ice-lolly shop would be very well patronised.

My first trip to a railway installation was on Wednesday 24 August 1955, when Eastleigh Locomotive Depot was visited. This was the beginning of my travels - you could say that it 'put steam into my blood' - and from that day, when I noted 86 'living steam' locos, I made up my mind to travel over some of the British Railways system and visit other depots, workshops and stations, just to see the many variations of steam engines common to their own particular region or area. This travelling would also widen my geographical knowledge of towns and cities in Great Britain.

As the years progressed from 1955 to 1968 - the latter year was to see the end of BR steam-hauled trains (except for the narrow-gauge Vale of Rheidol line in mid-Wales) - I travelled thousands of miles, spent hundreds of pounds on tickets and had the experience of sleeping all night on stations and trains. These trips took me and many of my friends to such places as Penzance, Fishguard, Dover, Manchester, Doncaster, Nottingham and Carnforth - the latter was to be the destination of my final trip before the demise of steam.

When making visits to railway installations I invariably had at least one enthusiast accompanying me. On some trips 'parties' were made up, these consisting of any number from four to 12 of us all travelling together. We travelled at reduced party rate whenever possible, which saved a considerable amount on fares. A party ticket for an excursion from Portsmouth Harbour station to Cardiff on a Sunday, for instance, would be collected from a local travel agent on the previous Friday or Saturday. Sometimes additional younger spotters would come along with our party on Sunday excursions, boosting the numbers up to 15 or 16.

I shall always have fond memories of the Class 'T9' 4-4-0s, nick-named 'Greyhounds', and the Class 'M7' 0-4-4 tanks which would be employed on the Eastleigh-Southampton-Andover Junction trains - the majority of these two classes were introduced before the turn of the century and were still doing yeoman service in the mid and late 1950s, having served during two World Wars! Other classes associated with Fratton spring to mind, of which some became extinct early in my train-spotting days, these being the Class 'N15X' 4-6-0s, more commonly known as the 'Remembrance' Class, and the Class 'H2' 4-4-2 'Atlantics'.

Also of note were the Class 'D15' 4-4-0s and the single Class 'S11' and 'S12' 4-4-0s, numbered 30400 and 30434 respectively. No 30400 worked from Guildford shed over the Reading to Redhill route and often made appearances at Fratton; withdrawn in 1954, it was the final one of a class of ten 4-4-0s. No 30434 also spent its final years shedded at Guildford and also worked the Reading to Redhill route, making the occasional visit to Fratton. This engine, like No 30400, out-lived all other

members of its class, which in all totalled 20. No 30434 was with-drawn in 1955.

The years 1957 to 1959 were the best remembered at Fratton engine shed, which carried the code 71D and later 70F. In those days the depot had a fair-sized allo-cation of 28 steam locomotives of various classes and designs. I don't ever recall the depot having any diesels in its allocation, but the 0-6-0 diesel shunters from Eastleigh could nearly always be noted in the vicinity of Fratton yard. The brick-built roundhouse-type depot with its 50-foot turntable and many lines leading off was unique, being the only completely covered roundhouse depot on the Southern Region. Similar ones were to be found at Guildford and Horsham, but these were only semi-roundhouses.

The local train-spotters grew up with Southern Region steam as their main interest, basically because these, apart from visiting Western Region engines and the newly introduced 'Standards', were the only types seen, but this was to change later and the Western was to overwhelm our loyalty to 'all things Southern'. The appearance of a Western Region steam locomotive, usually a 'Hall', at Fratton station at 11.30 am every weekday morning from Reading General was proba-bly the reason why Eddie Rooke and I took an interest in these very smart engines with their cop-per-capped chimneys and brass numberplates and nameplates.

Other Western Region classes, notably the 'Granges', 'Manors' and 'Moguls' (2-6-0s), could all be seen arriving on summer week-ends with ten or more carriages behind the tender forming excur-sions from such places as Gloucester, Birmingham, Swansea and Swindon. During a busy Saturday or Sunday in the hectic summer service, up to six or seven

Westerns could be noted 'on shed' at Fratton. These excursions nearly always terminated at Portsmouth Harbour station, where, soon after arrival, a Fratton-allocated Class 'E4' 0-6-2, an 'O2' 0-4-4 tank or a class 'C2X' 0-6-0 would couple on to the rear of the emptied excursion carriages and take them to the sidings at Fratton. Usually a 4- or 5-hour stay was enjoyed by the visitors to 'Sunny Southsea', as it was known, but some of the excursions were booked through to the Isle of Wight, which would include a coach tour to such places as Shanklin Chine, Sandown and Ventnor.

And so to the railway visits, which began in 1955 and ended in 1968, a span of 14 years. The following accounts give, I believe, a realistic picture of my own and my many friends' experiences over the years. Up until 1961 we took for granted that the steam-dominated power of BR was far from ending; in fact, not one of us would ever have dreamed that in August 1968 we would be seeing the last standard gauge steam-hauled passenger-carrying train on BR. The age of the diesel had now come, although it had been in the background for some years previously. None of us thought that steam power would be replaced so swiftly, particularly in the early 1960s when steam engines of the 'Standard' designs had only been built at Swindon Works in the late 1950s. In fact, the last engine built, No 92220 *Evening Star*, came out of the works new as late as March 1960.

All photographs in this book were, unless otherwise stated, taken by the author. All line drawings of locomotives were drawn by the author to give a rough indication of their appearance, and are not necessarily to scale and do not necessarily show all external details and fittings. Street maps and diagrams were also drawn by the author, and again represent only a rough indication and are not necessarily to scale.

All visits by rail described in this book start either from Fratton, Portsmouth & Southsea or Portsmouth Harbour stations. Some visits in later years were made by car or scooter, and these started from either Eddie's parents' house or my parents' house in Penhale Road, Fratton.

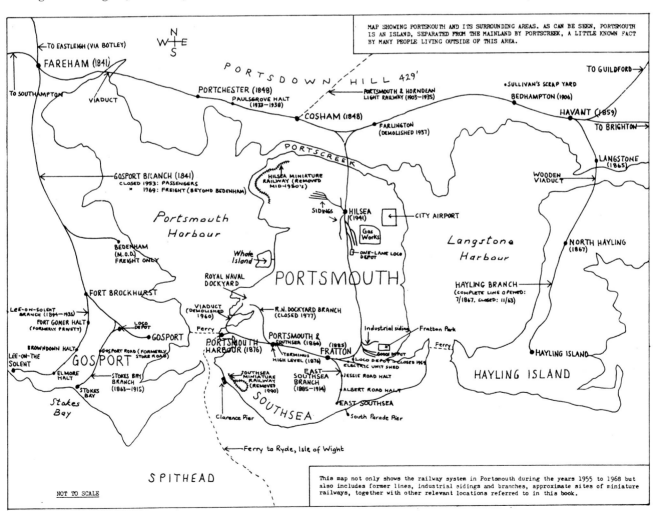

EASTLEIGH

WEDNESDAY 24 AUGUST

This was a half-day trip to Eastleigh and was the first of many visits to this locomotive depot which consisted of 15 roads, both ends being open. The coaling plant was at the side of the shed alongside Campbell Road, and the turntable was in full sight of the Waterloo to Southampton line at the front of the depot. Of the 88 locomotives 'on shed', only two were diesels, these being 0-6-0 shunters allocated here. Forty-three engines were carrying nameplates and were main-line types, while 16 tank engines of various classes, designs and wheel arrangements were noted.

The accompanying table gives a breakdown of the Southern Region classes seen, together with some relevant details. I did not recall seeing any withdrawn steam locomotives on the 'dead line' at the rear of the shed adjacent to the airport; the majority of those on shed were either in steam or just awaiting their respective duties.

Eastleigh, being the nearest main-line shed to Fratton, was of course visited many times during the period of this book. One of my most vivid recollections is of the many hours spent on Campbell Road bridge; this was extremely

Class	Wheels	Designer(s)	Introduced
'M7'	0-4-4	Drummond	1897 & 1903
'O2'	0-4-4	Adams	1889
'T9'	4-4-0	Drummond	1899 & 1900
'700'	0-6-0	Drummond	1897
'N15'	4-6-0	Maunsell/Urie	1918, 1925 & 1928
'H15'	4-6-0	Maunsell/Urie	1914 & 1924
'S15'	4-6-0	Urie	1920 & 1936
'Q'	0-6-0	Maunsell	1938
'V'	4-4-0	Maunsell	1930 & 1938
'U'	2-6-0	Maunsell	1928
'E1'	0-6-0	Stroudley	1874
'E4'	0-6-2	Billinton	1910
'N15X'	4-6-0	Billinton	1934
'WC'	4-6-2	Bulleid	1945
'BB'	4-6-2	Bulleid	1948
'MN'	4-6-2	Bulleid	1941 & 1951

71A EASTLEIGH DEPOT

Steam locomotives:

2214	30033	30117	30125	30130	30229	30283	30285	30313	30316	30331	30375	30376
30377	30449	30450	30455	30457	30475	30478	30479	30483	30499	30501	30505	30510
30535	30549	30701	30710	30739	30746	30748	30749	30750	30755	30774	30784	30785
30786	30788	30790	30839	30856	30864	30909	30932	31618	31619	31630	31805	32113
32327	32332	32559	32579	34010	34011	34012	34037	34041	34042	34043	34047	34066
34071	34081	34097	34099	34102	34103	35002	35009	35019	35020	35027	35029	42075
42102	73051	76007	76010	76025	76026	80016	82016					

Diesel locomotives:

13012   15231

88 locomotives on shed

popular with train-spotters, since it was ideally placed to watch movements in and out of the shed and the Works and its yard, on the Portsmouth line via Botley and, of course, the main Waterloo to Weymouth line. Expresses, many of them Boat Trains to and from the now defunct Southampton Ocean Terminal, were commonplace, and it was possible to see down expresses several miles up the line from the direction of Winchester as they approached at speeds well in excess of 70 mph.

Although I personally never did, many of my friends from Fratton regularly used to cycle to Eastleigh at weekends, a distance of nearly 23 miles, in the days before motorways when it was a lot safer and much more pleasurable to ride a cycle over such a distance.

This local trip to Eastleigh shed was made without a permit, but was successfully completed without being stopped by the Shed Foreman whose office was situated in close proximity to the coaling plant.

To sum up, a memorable first visit, with the accent very much on 'live' steam at a large and busy locomotive depot where a very

Below right Off shed and on duty. Class 'N15' ('King Arthur') 4-6-0 No 30748 *Vivien* awaits departure from platform 4 of Eastleigh station with the 5.27 pm 'workmens' train to Portsmouth & Southsea. This train was known by local railway enthusiasts as the 'workmens' although it was an ordinary service train - its departure time proved ideal for railwaymen who had just ended their working day at the nearby Locomotive Works, Carriage Works or engine shed. The 5.27 would stop at Botley, Fareham Portchester, Cosham, Fratton and finally Portsmouth & Southsea (Low Level). *Vivien* had recently emerged from Eastleigh Works after overhaul and repainting and, as can be seen from this photograph, was in excellent condition. She was being used on this train as a 'running-in' duty, prior to use on any main-line working. *E. C. Rooke*

Above Moving out - Class 'LN' ('Lord Nelson') 4-6-0 No 30856 *Lord St Vincent* moves slowly out of the yard. *E. C. Rooke*

Below Moving in - following the visit to the depot, un-rebuilt 'West Country' Class 4-6-2 No 34107 *Blandford Forum* was photographed entering the yard. *E. C. Rooke*

The locomotives carried this familiar emblem, the first crest to be introduced by British Railways in 1948.

wide selection of Southern Region classes were noted. It was my only visit of 1955.

The letter reproduced below, dated 12 July 1955, was received from Mr G. E. 'Jim' Jackson, Area Secretary of the South Hants group of the Ian Allan Locospotters Club. I did not take advantage of any visits to depots during 1955 or 1956 with the South Hants group, but commenced with a visit to Swindon Locomotive works on Friday 4 January 1957. A reproduction of my Membership Card and the Member's Reference Book appears on pages 18-20. My membership commenced as from 12 July 1955.

THE MODERNISATION PLAN, 1955

In 1955 my interest in railways had just begun, as I was only a 14-year-old schoolboy, and details of the early days have already been described in the Preface. The most important railway news of 1955 was the British Railways Modernisation Plan, many of the ideas of which were pre-war projects that had been shelved - the British Transport Commission believed that it would take almost 15 years to complete any such plan, as steam locomotives, in the form of the Class '9F' 2-10-0s and many other 'Standard' types, were still coming out of the workshops new in 1955.

Basically, modernisation meant the scrapping of steam power and the change to diesel and electric motive power, to colour light signals, to the building of new 'modern image' stations and the demolition of the old steam sheds, replacing them with diesel re-fuelling points and modern depots.

British Railways had, in 1955, only *seven* main-line diesel loco-

motives in use, but this was to increase rapidly by the late 1950s with the withdrawal of most of the older types of steam engine, quickly followed by those built at later dates; these included the 'Standards' that had seen less than ten years' service on BR, a very short life for any steam locomotive considering that, for example, some of Drummond's 'T9s' and 'M7s' had been introduced in the 1897-1900 period and were still in active service in the early 1960s.

The Modernisation Plan - a £1,240,000 project - began in 1955 and was to change the face of railways in Britain. As you read through this book and the subsequent volumes, the visits to depots and stations will gradually show less steam and more diesel. Many of us local railway enthusiasts did not bother to record all the diesel numbers whenever we made a visit to a depot or station as we found it to be an increasingly depressing scene. As mentioned in the Introduction, we never visualised that steam power would cease on BR in 1968.

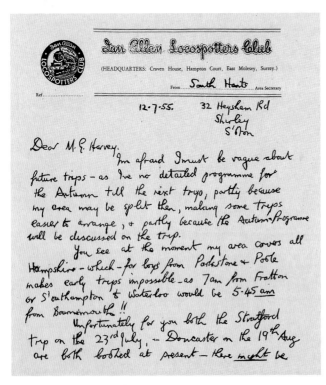

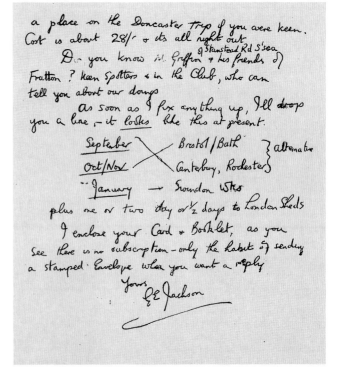

1956

FRATTON

SATURDAY 23 JUNE

The footbridge at Fratton station was visited from 11 am until 2.45 pm.

FRATTON			
Steam locomotives:			
4961	5952	6862	6864
6906	6929	30130	30747
30748	31611	31802	34009
34025	34069	75070	

The Western Region locomotives noted above were all employed on various excursion and through train services to Portsmouth Harbour station. One of the through services was the Wolverhampton train which travelled via Oxford, Reading West and Basingstoke.

As mentioned in the Introduction, Fratton station footbridge was an extremely popular spot with train-spotters, and it was not unusual for some of them to spend up to 12 hours there at weekends, interrupted only by visits to such establishments as the chip shop opposite the Talbot pub - 1d fritters a speciality! - or, in the summer months, the nearby general stores from where we purchased great numbers of ice-lollies. If we were lucky we were served by the owner's daughter, a very well-endowed young lady with red hair! At weekends when she was serving in the shop our consumption increased substantially!

Above Fratton station footbridge. Many a happy hour was spent at this spot.

Below Fratton railway station and surrounding area, 1956, showing locations of railway interest together with many other buildings and items, many of which are referred to elsewhere in this book.

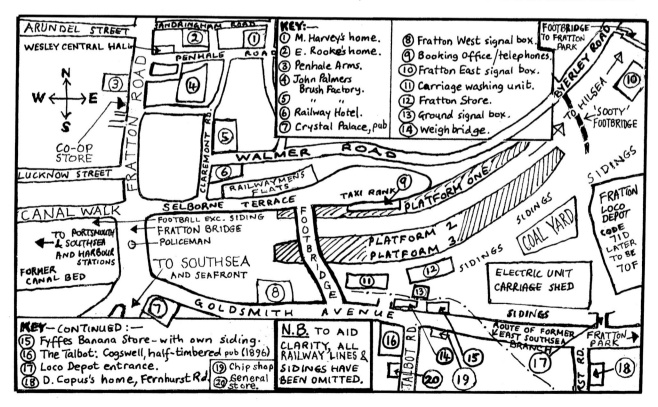

THE EAST SOUTHSEA BRANCH LINE

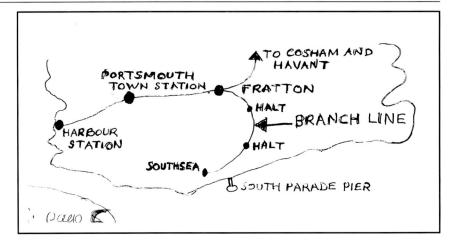

Fratton station opened in 1885, but was soon to be re-named Fratton & Southsea (1885-1905) to coincide with the opening of the East Southsea branch line. The present-day carriage washing unit occupies the former site of the branch-line platform. Drummond-designed steam railcars were used on this line which had two halts, Jessie Road and Albert Road, before the terminus at Southsea, just 1/4 mile from South Parade Pier. The last passenger train ran in 1914, due to the onset of the First World War. All available resources would be needed, and the branch was used for arms storage until its official closure in 1935.

SWINDON

WEDNESDAY 15 AUGUST

I was only 15 years old when I made my first ever visit to Swindon Locomotive Works. It was during the school holidays that I had made an application for a permit to visit the Works; my application was granted and a permit to admit four to the Works on Wednesday 15 August 1956 was received. I had already purchased a Southern Region local 'Runabout' ticket several days previously, and this took me to Andover Junction; the additional return fare (half fare) would have to be paid between Andover Junction and Swindon Junction.

The local enthusiasts who accompanied me on this trip were Tony Ingram, Jack Knowler, Ian Gray, Vic Copping, 'Podge' Brown and 'Bun'.

We were steam-hauled between Fratton and Andover Junction by a Fratton-allocated Class 'U' 2-6-0 locomotive - its number was not recorded. The route from Portsmouth to Swindon was via Fareham, Eastleigh, Chandlers Ford, Romsey, Stockbridge, Andover Town, Andover Junction, Marlborough, Swindon Town and finally to Swindon Junction.

Engine numbers noted on the forward and return journeys are not available, having been mislaid many years before compiling my original book.

The table opposite is a combined list of locomotives either being repaired, awaiting workshop attention, in the scrap yard or passing through the Junction station. Regrettably, in those earliest of my train-spotting days I did not have the foresight to categorise the numbers seen into specific locations.

From information received whilst on this visit, the following

Below left Class 'TV' (Taff Vale) 0-6-2 tank, introduced in 1924 and a Great Western rebuild with a superheated taper boiler of the Cameron TV 'A' Class, introduced in 1914. It was quite common on future visits to see one of this class being employed as a temporary shunter in the large Works yard, prior to it being cut up for scrap.

Below 'Star' Class 4-6-0.

SWINDON

Steam locomotives:

312	316	348	351	366	377	382	1001	1009	1017	1020	1023	1420
1428	1612	2203	2205	2276	2826	2832	2833	2840	2845	2853	2861	2880
2892	3659	3677	3724	3739	3746	3794	3812	3856	3859	4062	4079	4080
4088	4096	4377	4538	4651	4663	4909	4925	4927	4936	4972	4989	5001
5018	5019	5025	5042	5047	5049	5055	5065	5067	5087	5092	5094	5336
5533	5566	5742	5939	5954	5962	5989	5996	6001	6007	6012	6016	6018
6023	6026	6027	6104	6108	6131	6137	6138	6141	6156	6360	6394	6821
6823	6858	6971	6975	7006	7008	7013	7015	7016	7019	7020	7027	7035
7037	7242	7413	7435	7437	7740	7761	7805	7815	7816	7905	8401	8451
8461	8762	8779	9315	9415	9423	9469	9642	9740	9773	31843	41299	46507
46514	70020	70025	70026	70029	75005	75007	75021	78002	78007	82000	90565	92087

Diesel locomotives:
13003 15100 15102 15104

Gas-turbine locomotive:
18000

148 locomotives noted (none of which I had seen before, having previously only seen the occasional Western Region engine at Fratton)

Nos 312-382 inclusive were Class 'TV' 0-6-2 tanks (see drawing opposite)

No 4062 was a 'Star' Class 4-6-0, named *Malmesbury Abbey*. Introduced 1907. Churchward design. Only three of this class remained at the time of this visit. See illustration opposite.

No 31843 was a Southern Region Class 'N' 2-6-0. Introduced 1917. Maunsell mixed traffic design. Quite an unusual visitor to Swindon, being normally overhauled at either Eastleigh or Ashford (Kent) Works.

No 18000 was introduced 1949. Brown Boveri (Switzerland) design, built for Western Region in Switzerland. Passenger express type.

proved to be most interesting:
* During its peak periods of locomotive construction, the Works was able to complete two finished engines each week.
* Every year 1,000 locomotives were either repaired or overhauled.

To sum up, this was an enjoyable first visit, and numerous classes were noted 'in Works' in many different stages of repair, some completely stripped down to their frames, whilst others were ex-Works waiting in the yard for running-in duties. We had covered a very large area on foot and were glad to return to the station and catch the train home.

WESTBURY

FRIDAY 17 AUGUST

This visit followed up the Swindon visit of two days before, and I was once again accompanied by Vic Copping, 'Podge' Brown and 'Bun', together with my close friend Eddie Rooke who decided to come along. A visit to the depot and station was planned and some train-spotting beside the main line at Westbury.

BETWEEN FRATTON AND SALISBURY

Steam locomotives:
30162 30309 34103 42100
73025 73026 76064

With the others I had already purchased Southern Region local 'Runabout' tickets earlier in the week. These took us as far as Salisbury, where we all purchased half-fare day return tickets to Westbury.

The table overleaf is a combined list of locomotives noted on my first visit to Westbury depot (82D), Westbury station and on the main line.

WESTBURY

82 D

Steam locomotives:

1005	1433	2261	2808	2824	2827	2828	2836	2839	2868	2869	2883	3408
3614	3735	3815	4075	4203	4636	4701	4704	4917	4925	4927	4945	4958
5044	5048	5082	5314	5358	5391	5402	5403	5406	5419	5422	5423	5510
5554	5689	5701	5767	5953	6000	6004	6009	6010	6026	6107	6338	6341
6356	6399	6820	6822	6835	6876	6902	6915	6946	6966	6977	6994	7008
7024	7031	7748	7784	7917	7924	8744	9305	9628	48404	70024		

76 locomotives noted

Westbury depot, which was 'all-steam', was quite a neatly built structure containing four roads with a turntable at the rear and a one-road repair shop adjoining the main shed.

Our visit was an enjoyable one, and was done without a permit, but we managed to get round all right. We stayed on the station for quite a considerable length of time just watching the movements of trains and light engines which were travelling to and from the depot.

The most outstanding memories of this trip came from the varied selection of express steam locomotives travelling to and from London (Paddington) on the main line, which was situated some distance from Westbury station. I well remember the 'King', 'Castle' and 'Hall' Classes, to name but a few, that sped past us on that sunny August day. We stayed beside the main line for several hours, in which time we ate sandwiches and drank orange squash which we had brought with us. I always carried a cloth haversack with me containing food and drink and various other assortments such as a plastic mac, notebooks and biros. It seems a shame when I look back to those early days to find that I did not take any photographs of these engines. One of the 'King' Class 4-6-0s which we

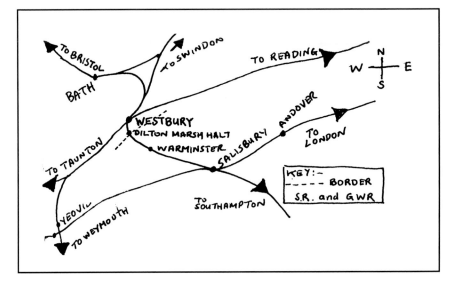

Westbury, Wilts, and its surrounding lines.

noted on the main line, No 6026 *King John*, had also been noted two days previously on our trip to Swindon.

No engine numbers were recorded on the homeward journey - we were all tired and dozed off. Our arrival back at Fratton was at 10 pm.

LONDON

SATURDAY 25 AUGUST

This was my first ever trip to London; we visited railway stations only, no locomotive depots.

A journey by rail in the 1950s and 1960s was always full of interest. There was no time to sit and read if one was to avoid missing

locomotives *en route* and on shunting duties in sidings which were commonplace at virtually every station in those days - a far departure from the modern-day scene. For example, on this trip to London it was necessary between Fratton and Havant (6¼ miles) to check Fratton shed yard and goods sidings, gaze with interest at the small industrial engines at Hilsea Gas Works, watch out to see what was shunting the Royal Ordnance

BETWEEN FRATTON AND WATERLOO VIA GUILDFORD

Steam locomotives:
30043 30086 30243 30246
30520 30675 30694 31549
31616 32506

Diesel locomotive:
15211

Right A Bulleid-designed Class 'Q1'. One of these unusual wartime design locomotives, No 33004, was noted on passing Guildford shed.

sidings at Hilsea, glance to see if anything was waiting on the Cosham triangle for us to pass (normally a Brighton to Plymouth steam-hauled train) and finally, on arrival at Havant, there was a chance to see one of the much-loved 'Terriers' in the bay platform awaiting departure for the Hayling Island branch line.

On our arrival at London (Waterloo) we immediately left the terminus and walked to

CHARING CROSS
Steam locomotives:
30902 30925

VICTORIA
Steam locomotives:
30794 31321 31789 34074 80012

PADDINGTON
Steam locomotives:
1503 1505 4954 4993 4997 5022 5085 5939 5994 6103 6110 6119 6120
6128 6136 6140 6146 6149 6160 6164 6165 6805 6843 6973 7002 7003
7017 7030 7036 7927 9412 9418 9420 9422 9705 9709 9710 70020 70026

EUSTON
Steam locomotives:
40021 40053 40066 40069 40208 41167 42302 42973 43045 44663 44676 44915 44950
45021 45249 45380 45392 45521 45532 45580 45583 45656 45733 46115 46120 46143
46200 46205 46257 47522 47527 47671 70033 80064 80065 80067

KING'S CROSS
Steam locomotives:
60003 60014 60025 60064 60134 60144 60500 60523 61139 61159 61393 67780 67790
67791 68902 68946 68986 69523 69527 69535 69536 69558 69569 69570 69572 69573
69575 69580 69586 69588 69593

LIVERPOOL STREET
Steam locomotives
61006 61160 61226 61252 61253 61270 61336 61360 61570 61573 61600 61630 61633
61636 61666 61670 61672 61951 67723 67730 67732 67737 68619 69520 69600 69614
69622 69636 69664 69667 69674 69688 69700 69702 69717 69723 69725 70003 70013

LONDON BRIDGE
Steam locomotives:
30905 30911 31509 34078 34086 34098 42106 75066

WATERLOO
Steam locomotives:
30132 30241 30242 30244 30321 30326 30699 31574 32487 32499 73114

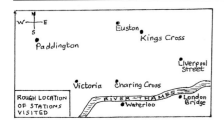

ROUGH LOCATION OF STATIONS VISITED

PASSING GUILDFORD DEPOT

Steam locomotives:
30027   30325   31799   32505

Charing Cross station across Hungerford Bridge spanning the River Thames. We had decided that the quickest way of travelling around London to visit stations would be to use London Transport tube trains, in preference to buses.

Waterloo was to be our final station of the visit before returning to Portsmouth.

We found this visit to London very exciting, noting many classes of steam engines new to us. No diesel locomotives were noted at any of the stations; in fact, the only one noted during the entire

trip was an 0-6-0 shunter near Guildford. We found that all the stations visited seemed to be 'alive with steam', and noted a continual activity at every location; whether it was a small suburban tank engine employed on carriage duties or a main-line express arriving or departing, it all added up to a very enjoyable day's visit to the capital.

It is of note that during 1956 the use of 3rd Class travel on British Railways was discontinued.

Although this book sets out to recollect my pursuit of the steam locomotive, some readers may find

the following list of SR electric unit numbers noted that day of interest:

WATERLOO: 4119, 4286, 4290, 4294, 4321, 4325, 4361, 4371, 4372, 4550, 4555, 4601, 4621, 4627, 4648, 4673, 4690, 4702, 4706, 4712, 4718, 4737, 5016, 5020, 5043, 5118, 5127, 5148, 5192, 5199, 5205 and 5225.

CHARING CROSS: 2619, 2655, 2678, 2927, 2952 and 5190.

VICTORIA: 3026, 4335, 4675, 4701, 5008, 5019, 5047, 5112, 5115, 5142, 5171, 5176, 5183, 5198, 5203, 5213, 5221, 5725, 5746 and 5752.

A total of 185 steam, one diesel and 58 SR electric unit numbers were noted.

1957

SWINDON

FRIDAY 4 JANUARY

I went on this organised visit to Swindon Works and Depot with the South Hants Locospotters Club (a branch of the Ian Allan Locospotters Club, whose headquarters were at Craven House, Hampton Court, East Molesey, Surrey). The South Hants area Secretary was 'Jim' Jackson from Shirley, Southampton, who always came along on all the organised trips with boys from the Poole, Bournemouth, Southampton and Portsmouth areas; sometimes even

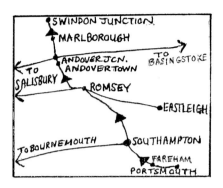

Route taken from Portsmouth to Swindon.

much older enthusiasts came along with him, so the age group was quite varied - anyone from about 12 years of age up to 40 was always welcome, as long as they were

interested in steam locomotives. The return fare was 10 shillings.

The table below is a combined list of locomotives under repair, awaiting Works, in the scrapyard, stock shed, locomotive depot and also at the Junction station. This was my second visit to the locomotive works, but my first visit to the depot.

Class 'RR' (Rhymney Railway) 0-6-2 tank No 35 was the most surprising 'cop' of the day. Originally from the Welsh valleys, it was noted in the scrapyard awaiting cutting up. This was a fast diminishing class, most of them at this date being sent here for cutting up. A total of 51 tank

SWINDON

Steam locomotives:

35	347	348	378	380	388	1000	1004	1006	1010	1012	1025	1028
1029	1365	1433	1454	1504	1658	2203	2208	2809	2818	2829	2865	2891
3666	3682	3684	3746	3763	3780	3835	3849	3864	4073	4076	4077	4082
4083	4086	4088	4091	4097	4099	4538	4582	4612	4647	4707	4918	4926
4930	4959	4962	5000	5007	5009	5013	5018	5025	5034	5039	5042	5048
5052	5054	5056	5058	5069	5072	5073	5084	5087	5092	5094	5095	5096
5311	5338	5351	5399	5509	5538	5800	5802	5804	5922	5923	5958	5968
6015	6021	6025	6028	6115	6123	6129	6312	6320	6326	6367	6373	6379
6381	6639	6699	6741	6805	6818	6841	6850	6860	6873	6909	6912	6955
6961	6965	6966	6973	6974	6999	7005	7006	7014	7015	7017	7025	7026
7027	7031	7309	7409	7415	7424	7700	7792	7794	7801	7808	7905	7914
7917	7923	8433	8472	8783	8793	9315	9407	9451	9600	9604	9672	9720
9721	9795	46509	70020	70023	70027	73012	75000	75006	75025	75026	75027	75028
75053	75054	75055	78000	78003	82007	92004	92007	92093	92094			

Diesel locomotives:
13102 15104 15231

Gas-turbine locomotive:
18000

183 locomotives noted

engines of many designs were noted, and over 70 main-line steam locomotives. Only three diesels were seen, these all being 0-6-0 shunters. The gas-turbine No 18000 had been observed on my previous visit.

I kept my Ian Allan Locospotters Club Membership Card and Member's Reference Book which had been sent to me by 'Jim' Jackson, and they are reproduced here to give some idea of how young railway enthusiasts were encouraged to share their interests by joining this kind of local group.

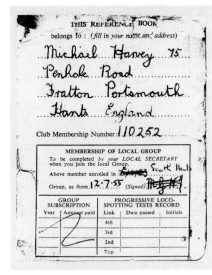

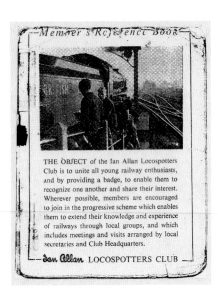

THE OBJECT of the Ian Allan Locospotters Club is to unite all young railway enthusiasts, and by providing a badge, to enable them to recognize one another and share their interest. Wherever possible, members are encouraged to join in the progressive scheme which enables them to extend their knowledge and experience of railways through local groups, and which includes meetings and visits arranged by local secretaries and Club Headquarters.

Ian Allan LOCOSPOTTERS CLUB

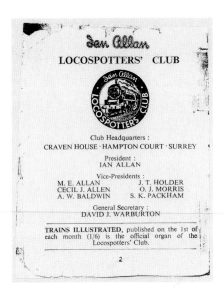

Ian Allan
LOCOSPOTTERS' CLUB

Club Headquarters :
CRAVEN HOUSE · HAMPTON COURT · SURREY

President :
IAN ALLAN

Vice-Presidents :

M. E. ALLAN	J. T. HOLDER
CECIL J. ALLEN	O. J. MORRIS
A. W. BALDWIN	S. K. PACKHAM

General Secretary :
DAVID J. WARBURTON

TRAINS ILLUSTRATED, published on the 1st of each month (1/6) is the official organ of the Locospotters' Club.

2

The Club Rule

Members of the Club are free to enjoy the hobby in any way they like, provided they do not break the Law and endanger the good name of the Club. Thus we have only one rule, but we take good care to see that it is kept. The rule of the Locospotters Club is :

Members of the Club will not in any way interfere with railway working or material, nor be a nuisance or hindrance to their staff, nor, above all, trespass on railway property. No one will be admitted a member of the Club unless he solemnly agrees to keep this rule.

The Railways are doing a great deal to help us enjoy our spotting to the full, and it is up to us to see that this consideration is not abused.

National and local officials of the Club are empowered to take immediate action against any member found to be breaking the Rule.

3

ABOUT LOCOSPOTTING .....

POSSIBLY you already know all there is to know about British Railways and its locomotives, in which case this part of the Reference Book will not be of much importance for you. On the other hand, many members are enrolled when their interest in the subject has only just begun, and they are anxious to know how to make the most of it, and to learn more about it. In case you are one of these, the following notes may help you.

MAKING SENSE OUT OF NUMBERS

If your Locospotting is to be just writing down every loco. number you see without bothering what the type of loco. is or where it comes from, you will pretty soon get tired of the whole thing. You might just as well write down the numbers of houses as you walk along the street! Locospotting gets interesting when you are trying to complete your set of one "class" (and despite scrapping and "standardization," there are still hundreds of different classes left). The next stage is to look out for the shed code (a small plate on the smokebox door bearing a number followed by a letter, e.g. 7C: Holyhead: see illustration), and this enables you to trace where the engine belongs. By so doing many really keen Locospotters discover some very interesting " through workings " of locomotives, and with the help of the "ABC Locoshed Book," keep their records of loco. allocations up-to-date.

4

FACTS ABOUT BRITISH RAILWAYS

Space doesn't allow us to tell you all about the history of our railways here, but you should do your best to find out all about your favourite systems from books and from older enthusiasts. Suffice it to say for the present that our railways were started by a number of relatively small companies towards the middle of the last century, and for the first fifty years there was fierce competition between rival systems. The number of companies was gradually reduced as a result, many smaller concerns being absorbed with their more powerful competitors. In 1923 the " Grouping " took place, and almost all the existing companies were merged by Act of Parliament into the four big main-

5

line Companies whose names are still familiar to us : the Great Western, Southern, London Midland & Scottish, and the London & North-Eastern. Of these, only the Great Western had survived from the pre-Grouping days.

In 1947 these companies were taken over by the state and their administration handed to the Railway Executive of the British Transport Commission, who adopted the words " British Railways " as their popular title. This authority now controls all the standard (4' 8½") gauge railways in Britain, and administers them through six Regions. These Regions have their own regional colours to which the six Club badges correspond, and their territories have been formed from those of the old main-line companies with certain alterations.

DO YOU KNOW YOUR REGIONS ?

When British Railways took control on 1st January, 1948, the old four main-line companies (G.W.R., S.R., L.M.S.R. and L.N.E.R.) ceased to exist. But the railways of Britain are too big to run from one centre, so that six Regions were created to administer the traffic in future. These Regions are based on the lines covered by the four companies which they superseded, with certain alterations. Broadly speaking, the rearrangement was as follows :

The G.W.R. became the Western Region :

The S.R. became the Southern Region ;

6

The L.M.S.R. (South of Scottish border) became the London Midland Region ;

The L.N.E.R. (South of Doncaster and Barnsley) became the Eastern Region ;

The L.N.E.R. (North of Doncaster and South of the Scottish border) became the North-Eastern Region ;

The L.M.S.R. and L.N.E.R. (North of Scottish Border) became the Scottish Region.

Since the change-over, a number of lines have changed from one region to another, in order to simplify organization and eliminate overlapping territories. The most important of these include the ex-Great Central main line from Marylebone (London) to Manchester, which has been transferred from the Eastern to the Western Region in the London Area, and to the London Midland Region farther north ; the ex-Midland Birmingham-Bristol line which has gone to the Western, and the Southern lines west of Exeter, which have become Western Region responsibility also.

HOW THE NUMBERS CAME ABOUT

Although the highest B.R. loco. number you will see is 92029, there aren't nearly 100,000 locos. in service. The British Railways numbering system covers a large range and has many gaps, because it was formed by generally adding fixed amounts to the existing numbers according to the railway company to which they had belonged, thus eliminating duplication. The system used was as follows :

7

Now You are a Locospotter !

Three views of a Locospotter's ambition realized. *Left upper :* Members visit a long-closed Welsh branch line and ride in open trucks (the only stock available !) *Above :* Being shown " the works " on a Club special visit. *Left lower :* Starting work on the railway, as hundreds of members have done.

8

9

---

1. Former G.W.R. locomotives retained their original numbers, between 1 and 9999.

2. Diesel locomotives of all regions were re-numbered in the series 10000-19999. Gas turbine locos. built later have also been included in this series.

3. Electric locomotives of all regions were re-numbered in the series 20000-29999.

4. Former Southern Railway locomotives were mainly re-numbered by the addition of 30000 to their existing numbers, so that these are now included in the series 30000-39999.

5. Former L.M.S. locomotives were mainly re-numbered by the addition of 40000 to their existing numbers so that these are now included in the series 40000-59999.

6. Former L.N.E.R. locomotives were mainly re-numbered by the additon of 60000 to their existing numbers, so that these are now included in the series 60000-69999.

7. The numbers 70000-89999 were reserved for B.R. standard locomotives, of which the main types have already appeared.

8. Former Ministry of Supply " Austerity " locomotives taken over by British Railways or their predecessors were re-numbered in the series beginning 90000.

10

WHAT TO DO NOW YOU HAVE JOINED

Would you like to be a " Progressive Locospotter " ?

" Progressive Locospotting " is what we call the new scheme of local group membership which is now being tried in nearly all the Club's groups. You can start on the scheme straight away by joining the Group organized by your nearest Club local Secretary. By learning certain interesting facts about railways and carrying out certain tests and qualifications, you can reach your first step on the " Progressive Locospotting " ladder. This means you are a " Fourth Link " Locospotter, and you will receive a certificate from Headquarters confirming this. You can also buy a special metal locomotive badge bearing the words " Fourth Link."

The idea of the " Links " is borrowed from railwaymen's vocabulary. As you may know, there are several " links " at each shed, and drivers work their way progressively to the " Top Link," in which they drive all the fastest expresses worked by their shed. In " Progressive Locospotting," there are four links : Fourth, Third, Second and Top. The normal time which must elapse between each test is 3 months, so that you become a " Top Link " Locospotter after not less than one year's membership. These periods can be varied in special circumstances, and one factor is your behaviour on Club occasions, which, if good, can get you on quickly, and, if not so good, can have the opposite effect !

11

The final stage is to become a " Senior Locospotter," a position open to all " Top Link " Locospotters after they have passed their 13th birthday. A special test for Senior Membership is to produce an exercise on any particular branch of railway practice or operation which especially interests you. In future, " Organizing Assistants "—members who show ability in helping to organize Group events, will be recruited from the Senior Locospotters, and in due course, when a vacancy occurs, they will have a chance to become Group Secretaries.

How do the Local Groups Work ? The Club's groups are mainly under the control of a number of voluntary adult helpers, called " Area Secretaries." In some places, they run the groups directly themselves, and in others they do so through Group Secretaries. Although there are by no means enough adult helpers to make it possible to have a permanent group in every town, it is usually possible for the keenest members to join in the activities arranged by the Area Secretary. These activities, apart from helping you to learn everything you need to know about railways in connection with " Progressive Locospotting," also include frequent visits to places of railway interest, such as works, sheds, etc. Not all Secretaries have been able to arrange indoor accommodation for regular meetings, but most are trying to do so, and in the meantime your " Progressive Locospotting " programme will be carried out as far as possible during outdoor meetings and on journeys in connection with visits.

Group Subscriptions. Most groups have a small

12

---

subscription covering notification of events and other expenses. Those not meeting regularly usually charge 1/6 annually for postal notification, and an additional charge is made to cover expenses for each meeting or visit.

NOTE : *A list of Area Secretaries is enclosed with this booklet*, so that you can find your nearest Secretary and contact him for details of group activities in your district. If you are not sure whom to write to, send to the General Secretary at Craven House, Hampton Court, Surrey (enclosing S.A.E.) and he will advise you.

" Progressive Locospotting " is being run by the Area Secretaries and their assistants in their spare time. Club H.Q. are always happy to advise on the scheme, but we are not in a position to require any Secretary to carry out any of its provisions if circumstances make it impossible for him to do so, nor can we undertake to operate the scheme direct by correspondence.

The Large-Scale Trips. These are arranged by Club Headquarters during the school holidays, and consist mainly of visits to big railway Works, with special trains or cheap fare facilities from the main centres, such as London, Birmingham, Manchester, Leeds, etc. These are normally held on mid-week days, as large-party facilities are not usually provided by the railways at week-ends.

Details of these events are given in the Ian Allan monthly rail-news magazine " Trains Illustrated " (see page 16), but you can receive information by

13

post about the events affecting your area by joining our Mailing List. To do so, send a minimum of **four** stamped addressed envelopes (1½d. stamps) to the General Secretary. When the last is used you will be advised so that you can send some more envelopes. Envelopes should not be smaller than 3½" x 4½".

A Note to Older Members, Parents, and anyone interested in encouraging Intelligent Interest in Railways : We are in great need of adult enthusiasts' help in running our local activities. If you can spare even a little of your time for the arranging of events for members, the General Secretary will be very pleased to hear from you. *Members aged 16 or over* can be of great help as Group Secretaries or assistants to adult organizers. If you are in this category, the General Secretary will be pleased to hear from you, too.

14

POINTS TO NOTE

● The General Secretary is always pleased to help as far as he can with members' queries, but he cannot guarantee a reply if no stamped addressed envelope is enclosed.

● Always remember that you CANNOT enter any railway property without permission. Your membership of the Club does not entitle you to enter a station without a ticket or a loco. depot without a permit. Note that the Club *cannot* issue permits, and that British Railways normally only issue them to adults. If you are too young to get a permit yourself you can still visit sheds by joining your local Group (see previous page) and taking part in visits arranged by its Secretary.

● **Membership Card, etc.** You should have received with this booklet your membership card and the badge or badges you asked for. If you lose your Card you can obtain a replacement by sending a 6d. Postal Order and stamped addressed envelope. Quote your membership number if you remember it. You can also obtain replacement or extra badges at 6d. each, details of colours being given on the Member's Order Form, a copy of which is enclosed.

● Orders for books and Club materials can most conveniently be placed by using the Member's Order Form, which should be completed according to the instructions. With all orders for BOOKS of 1/- or more in value placed on an Order Form, you are given Purchase Vouchers (P.V.'s) which you can use to pay part or all of the cost of subsequent

15

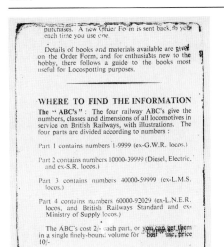

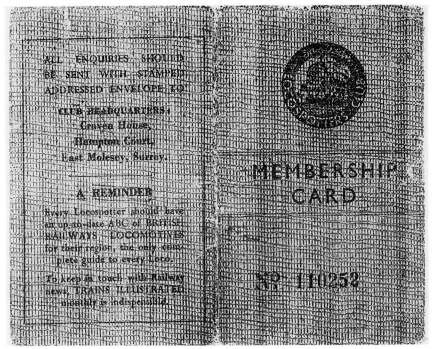

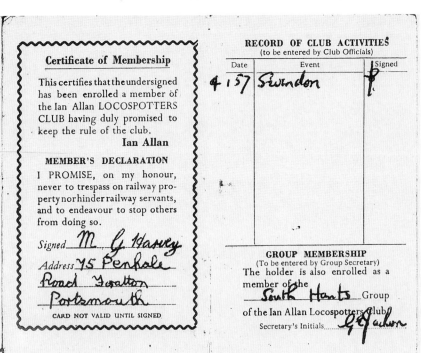

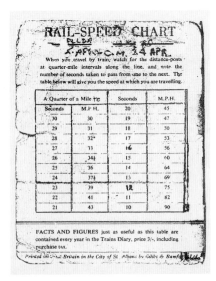

After reading through this *Member's Reference Book*, you now have an idea of how young railway enthusiasts were encouraged to join in and share the activities of a Locospotters Club. Many adults assumed that locospotting consisted of a visit to a railway station and writing some numbers in a notebook, nothing else being achieved - but this was all wrong. Many boys had, through train-spotting, become very interested in railways in general, and some had even made their life-long career a railway job, while others today are very active in the field of steam railway preservation.

Visits such as this one to Swindon Locomotive Works

proved to be extremely interesting, actually seeing engines stripped to their frames and in various other stages of overhaul. Some were noted in 'ex-Works' condition, 'the finished product' waiting in the Works yard with their gleaming paintwork, brass numberplates and nameplates and copper-capped chimneys. Ex-Works locomotives were often used on 'running-in' turns on local trains from Swindon before being returned to their depot of allocation.

EASTLEIGH

SATURDAY 19 JANUARY

This was a half-day visit to Eastleigh Locomotive Works. Departure from Fratton was at about 1 pm and the return fare was 5/3d. This was my first visit to the Works.

A Class '757' 0-6-2 tank locomotive was seen in Eastleigh Works scrapyard.

OPEN DAYS AT THE WORKS

These were held every summer and were extremely popular, with railway orphanages benefiting from the entrance proceeds. Occasions such as these were normally the only chance I got to get into the Works without first obtaining a permit. It was very difficult to 'bunk' (make an illegal entry to) this Works; some friends claimed that it was simple to enter on a Sunday morning from the rear, although they were frequently ejected without completing their visit. With the aid of the railway journals of the time, we were often able to identify dates on which railway societies were visiting the Works (as on this visit) and we would endeavour to accompany them.

EASTLEIGH WORKS

Steam locomotives:

2214	7312	30045	30061	30069	30102	30111	30212	30223	30306	30318	30325	30332
30451	30501	30509	30519	30536	30540	30707	30712	30738	30748	30765	30766	30770
30771	30783	30785	30786	30787	30824	30828	30853	30861	31619	31636	32655	33020
34009	34018	34028	34033	34037	34050	34052	34078	34093	35003	35012	35021	35022
35026	42077	73049	73087	73111	73112	75070	75074	76064	76069	80011	80018	82013
82014												

66 locomotives in Works

EASTLEIGH WORKS SCRAPYARD

Steam locomotive:
30758

This was a Class '757' 0-6-2 tank, introduuced 1907 to a Hawthorn Leslie design especially for Plymouth Docks and South Western Joint Railway branch lines. Named *Lord St Levan*. There were only two engines in this class, the other being No 30757 *Earl of Mount Edgcumbe*. At the date of this visit, No 30758 was waiting to be cut up for scrap.

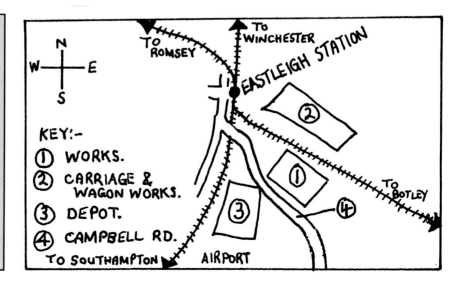

Preserved Adams-designed Class 'T3' 4-4-0 No 563 stands proudly on display in the Works yard during the 1957 Open Day. Note the steam crane and 0-6-0 diesel shunter on left, whilst on the far right is the coal bunker of Standard Class '4' 2-6-4 tank No 80016. *E. C. Rooke*

EASTLEIGH LOCOMOTIVE WORKS

The following information might be of interest. The Works were originally at Nine Elms, London, but moved down to Eastleigh in 1910 to occupy about 30 acres of land south of the railway station. At its height it employed about 1,900 people. The very first steam locomotive outshopped from the Works was No 101, a Class 'S14' tank, in October 1910. For the next 51 years the repairs, general overhaul and building of steam locomotives at the Works continued, and many famous classes were produced.

Whilst in this area it is also worth noting the Campbell Road area. As can be seen on the map, this road runs between the Works and the depot and contained neat brick-built houses especially erected for railwaymen who had previously been employed at the Nine Elms location - and, of course, men from many other locations who moved here. The move 'south' to the green countryside of Hampshire in the early 1900s must have been a complete contrast in living environment for these people.

A single railway line was laid along the bed of Campbell Road to assist in the construction of the workshops and the depot buildings. It was eventually replaced by the road which we see today. A feature of this area is the enormous amount of spiked railings used to divide the depot and Works boundaries, which gave it the name 'Spike Island'.

LONDON

SATURDAY 23 FEBRUARY

This was my first trip to London to visit locomotive depots. It was an organised trip with the South Hants Locospotters Club, run by Mr 'Jim' Jackson. The letter reproduced here was received from Mr Jackson giving information on this and other forthcoming visits which were organised by the Southampton area of the Ian Allan Locospotters Club, of which I was member No 110252.

Our departure from Fratton was on the 5.32 am, a 'workmens' train to London (Waterloo) stopping at all stations and halts on the way, arrival time at Waterloo being 7.48 am.

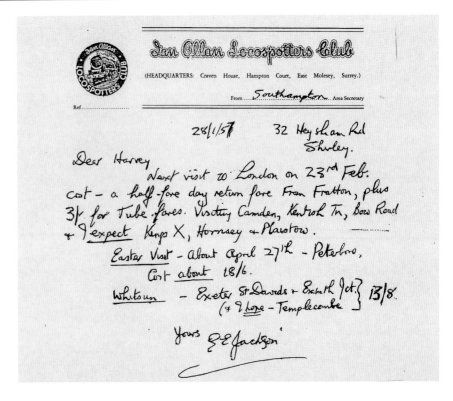

Ian Allan Locospotters Club

(HEADQUARTERS: Craven House, Hampton Court, East Molesey, Surrey.)

From *Southampton* Area Secretary

Ref...............

28/1/57   32 Heysham Rd
                      Shirley.
Dear Harvey
        Next visit to London on 23rd Feb.
Cost - a half-fare day return fare from Fratton, plus
3/- for Tube fares. Visiting Camden, Kentish Tn, Bow Road
+ I expect Kings X, Hornsey + Plaistow.
        Easter Visit - About April 27th - Peterboro.
        Cost about 18/6.
Whitsun - Exeter St Davids + Exmth Jct. 13/8
                (+ I hope - Templecombe)
        Yours E E Jackson

When travelling from Portsmouth to London or Brighton we were usually conveyed by electric units of the 2BIL type. These two-coach units, introduced between 1935 and 1938, totalled 162 in all. There being no gangway connection between carriages, each carriage had a lavatory; thus 2-BIL stood for *2*-coach, *bi-lavatory*. Seating capacity was 24 1st Class and 84 3rd Class. The livery was green.

By catching this early train we saved a considerable amount of money on a return fare, as we travelled at 'workmens' rate. On arrival at Petersfield (a quarter of the way to London) we would alight from the train, quickly dash through the subway to the down platform and purchase return

tickets from Petersfield to Waterloo, before returning to the waiting train. This procedure was necessary because the 'workmens' tickets were only issued for a certain number of miles from the issuing station, in this case Fratton to Petersfield. It would in fact have been possible to purchase a 'workmens' from Fratton to as far as Esher (on the outskirts of London) but that would have meant purchasing a ticket for the remaining part of the journey at normal rates; in addition, at that time of the morning trains would have been packed with London-bound commuters and getting a seat would have been impossible.

On our arrival at Waterloo (on time) we travelled by tube train to Chalk Farm from where we walked

BETWEEN GUILDFORD AND WATERLOO

Steam locomotives :

30055	30123	30124	30242
30248	30320	30322	30326
30349	30580	30692	30697
32476	32498	32499	32506
33001	33004	42100	80011

Diesel locomotives:

13270	13271	15214

the short distance to our first depot of the visit, Camden. This was a straight shed together with a turntable. Space was very limited and the engines listed in the table almost filled the shed and yard. It was quite a grimy depot.

CAMDEN DEPOT

Steam locomotives:

44759	44829	44867	44905	44935	45071	45269	45404	45505	45532	45533	45545	45592
45601	45603	45623	45630	45653	45676	46100	46114	46118	46136	46140	46142	46144
46150	46153	46205	46209	46210	46238	46249	46250	46253	46256	46257	47358	47668
47669	47671	47676	70049									

Diesel locomotives:
12052   12055

45 locomotives on shed

A famous steam locomotive, noted for the first time, was No 46100 *Royal Scot*, a Class '7P' 4-6-0 built at Glasgow in 1927. From information noted below its nameplate, *Royal Scot* was exhibited at Chicago in 1933 and then toured the USA and Canada, covering 11,194 miles. We noted nine of this class at Camden depot and another one at Kentish Town. All the 'Scots' were Stanier designed and they all carried nameplates.

KENTISH TOWN DEPOT

Steam locomotives:

40021	40028	40029	40030	40031	40035	40038	40040	40092	42156	42157	42237	42587
42590	42610	42617	42686	43919	44013	44029	44531	44532	44817	44944	44983	45058
45253	45279	45573	45575	45579	45612	45615	45627	45650	45682	45683	45712	46160
47200	47202	47260	47642	73046	73076	80099						

46 locomotives on shed

We then continued by tube train to our next depot of the visit, Kentish Town.

Visits to St Pancras and King's Cross stations were made prior to our next depot visit, Hornsey, which was in the north London suburbs. This was my first visit to St Pancras.

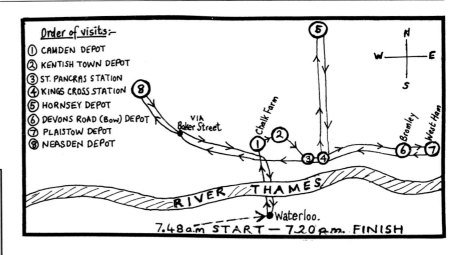

Order of visits:—
① CAMDEN DEPOT
② KENTISH TOWN DEPOT
③ ST. PANCRAS STATION
④ KINGS CROSS STATION
⑤ HORNSEY DEPOT
⑥ DEVONS ROAD (BOW) DEPOT
⑦ PLAISTOW DEPOT
⑧ NEASDEN DEPOT

VIA Baker Street • Chalk Farm • Bromley • West Ham

RIVER THAMES

→ Waterloo.

7.48 a.m START — 7.20 p.m. FINISH

ST PANCRAS

Steam locomotives:
40167 42374 42510 42704
42792 45626 45656 47204

Leaving the station, we made the 2-minute walk along Euston Road to King's Cross station.

KING'S CROSS

Steam locomotives:
60008 60055 60130 60853
61251 61603 67761 69523
69532 69541

We then caught a local train from King's Cross to Hornsey, purchasing half-fare return tickets.

On our arrival at Hornsey station we made the 5-minute walk via the footbridge to the depot entrance. This was an eight-lane,

BETWEEN KING'S CROSS AND HORNSEY

Steam locomotives :
60505 60821 61097 61142
61393 67746 67780 67791
67793 68862 68986 69493
69495 69513 69522 69528
69534 69543 69549 69569
69571 69573 69577 69583
69591

Diesel locomotives:
12138 13158

brick-built straight shed with a block end. At this date Hornsey's previous large allocation of 'J52' saddle tanks had almost been

BETWEEN HORNSEY AND KING'S CROSS

Steam locomotives:
60007 60022 60119 68862
69497 69654

Nos 60007/22 were Class 'A4' 4-6-2 locomotives introduced in 1935 to Gresley's streamlined design. No 60007 was named *Sir Nigel Gresley*; No 60022 *Mallard* is the locomotive that holds the world speed record for a steam-hauled train, 126 mph achieved in 1938 near Grantham, which remains unbeaten. This was the first time that I had noted No 60022, with her commemorative plaque which read: 'On 3rd July 1938 this locomotive attained a world speed record for steam traction of 126 miles per hour.'

34B HORNSEY DEPOT

Steam locomotives:
64233 64253 67741 68808 68824 68846 68866 68875 68894 68903 68907 68918 68920
68921 68929 68930 68931 68936 68945 68946 68949 68961 68966 68968 68971 68972
68979 68982 68983 68985 68989 68990 68991 69462 69477 69492 69499 69501 69502
69505 69530 69531 69533 69540 69545 69550 69554 69555 69556 69560 69566 69567
69573 69579 69587 69615 69618 69629 90034

Diesel locomotives:
12129 13310

61 locomotives on shed

Mallard - noted for the first time.

replaced by the Class 'J50' tanks, of which 25 were on shed.

Leaving the depot, we then returned to King's Cross, then to Bromley (District line) for our next depot of the visit, Devons Road (Bow), a brick-built ten-road block-end shed.

Continuing by District line to West Ham, we alighted and made the 10-minute walk to Plaistow depot, entering via the Holland Road gate. Plaistow was another block-end shed, consisting of eight roads; it was brick-built.

We travelled by tube train from Plaistow to King's Cross then via Baker Street to Neasden, which was to be our final depot visit (see table overleaf). Neasden shed was a six-road, brick-built, dead-end building, with a very long yard.

Leaving Neasden, we made the long tube train journey back to

BETWEEN PLAISTOW AND NEASDEN

Steam locomotives:
60104   67792

Waterloo, travelling via King's Cross and Holborn. Having time to purchase a drink and some food, we then caught the 8.50 pm electric unit train to Portsmouth.

These units consisted of 12 carriages, made up of three four-carriage corridor motor units - 4-CORs - number series 3101 to 3158. Known as the 'Nelsons', they were the mainstay of the Portsmouth direct line at this date. The journey took 90 minutes.

This was my second trip with 'Jim' Jackson and the South Hants

---

DEVONS ROAD (BOW) DEPOT

Steam locomotives:
41977	42223	42302	43000	43001	43020	44160	44381	47007	47219	47241	47302	47304
47310	47315	47483	47486	47488	47495	47499	47501	47514	47518	47559	47560	47561
58857	58859	80104

Diesel locomotive:
12049

30 locomotives on shed

No 41977 was a Class '3P' 4-4-2T 'Atlantic' tank, introduced in 1923. (See also Nos 41948/50/78 in the Plaistow table.)
Nos 58857/9 were Class '2F' 0-6-0 tanks, introduced in 1879 to Park's North London design.

PLAISTOW DEPOT

Steam locomotives:
41948	41950	41978	41982	41984	41985	41990	41991	41992	41993	42220	42516	42517
42523	42531	42681	42684	42687	44243	47312	47484	61233	68549	68656	69691	69695
69698	80070	80074	80075	80096	80097	80098	80132	80134	90196

36 locomotives on shed

NEASDEN DEPOT

Steam locomotives:
42222 42225 42230 42231 42232 42248 42250 42252 45381 60878 61116 61136 61206
67752 67758 67762 67778 67781 67783 67794 67796 69257 69319 69341 73155 73156
73157 73158 73159 76036 76041 80140 80142

Diesel locomotive:
11155

34 locomotives on shed

The Standard Class '5' 4-6-0s Nos 73155 to 73159 were designed at Doncaster and had just arrived at this depot new from Doncaster Works. They looked really immaculate with their gleaming black paintwork, lined-out in red and cream. Whether they were in steam or had been towed from Doncaster was not recorded, but they were all together in the yard. In appearance this class was very similar to the Stanier 'Black Fives'; in fact, they even incorporated features from them, a class which had proved very successful both on passenger and freight workings since their introduction in 1934.

Locospotters Club, and my first ever visit to London depots. It proved to be quite exhausting - many miles were travelled on both tube and suburban trains, with six depots being visited, permits for all of which were supplied by the Club. Only 11 diesels were noted, these all being shunters, while both Kentish Town and Plaistow were 'all-steam' sheds. Just about every class of steam locomotive allocated to the depots visited were noted, classes ranging from those introduced in the 1890s right up to Standard Class '5s' that were still being delivered.

In conclusion, it is worth noting that 102 SR electric unit numbers were noted on the forward journey alone! The majority were seen between Guildford and Waterloo. Two-carriage units were also noted, but the main numbers were the Bulleid-designed four-carriage suburban units built in the 1940s. It may be of interest to some readers to include these:
1861, 1863, 1864, 1869, 1874, 2926, 2930, 2936, 2951, 3007, 3008, 3012, 3026, 4103, 4108, 4109, 4110, 4119, 4121, 4130, 4143, 4283, 4290, 4297, 4305, 4307, 4311, 4313, 4315, 4322,

4327, 4331, 4335, 4340, 4343, 4345, 4346, 4358, 4361, 4362, 4363, 4366, 4378, 4383, 4505, 4507, 4510, 4517, 4607, 4621, 4622, 4628, 4630, 4635, 4637, 4640, 4643, 4646, 4656, 4667, 4668, 4671, 4673, 4674, 4675, 4680, 4681, 4694, 4697, 4699, 4700, 4703, 4704, 4706, 4715, 4717, 4723, 4728, 4738, 4739, 4740, 4741, 4742, 4743, 5025, 5035, 5037, 5043, 5044, 5112, 5133, 5143, 5170, 5175, 5181, 5192, 5213, 5219, 5225, 5227 and 5251. Electric Pullmans: 'Daphne', 'June', 'Lorna' and 'May'.

BRIGHTON AND LEWES

THURSDAY 13 APRIL

I departed from Fratton station on the 11.58 am electric train to Brighton in the company of a few enthusiasts from Fratton station footbridge. The return fare was 8/3d (6/- to Brighton).

This was my first ever visit to Brighton. The station opened in 1883, and the start of 1933 saw the first electric unit trains. The station was called Brighton Central until 1935. It has ten platforms, all of varying lengths; the Portsmouth and Littlehampton trains usually occupy platforms 1 and 2. At the date of this visit, some notings made at the station showed that trains ran to Plymouth, Bournemouth West, Cardiff, Leicester, Sheffield, Birmingham and Birkenhead on the Summer service.

On our arrival at Brighton we

FRATTON AREA

Steam locomotives:
30500 31804 31809 32509
32661 76066

purchased return tickets to Lewes, but before catching the train to Lewes we decided to visit the engine shed. We made the 10-minute walk via Terminus Road which runs parallel to the railway, and on nearing the top of this

BETWEEN CHICHESTER AND BRIGHTON

Steam locomotives:
DS680 DS681 30803 31724
32341 32351 32437 32438
32481 32484 32485 80010
80032 80152

Electric locomotive:
20002

DS680 and DS681, Class 'A1' and 'A1X' respectively, were both sighted on passing Lancing Carriage Works sidings. Lancing Works opened in 1905 and in its early days carriage and wagon building was transferred from Brighton main works. The finishing and painting was still done at Brighton, then coaches were given a coat of grey lead paint at Lancing and then towed to Brighton to be 'finished off'.

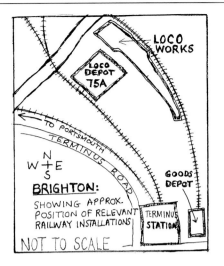

BRIGHTON: SHOWING APPROX. POSITION OF RELEVANT RAILWAY INSTALLATIONS. NOT TO SCALE

minus station, access via the end of the platform was 'dangerous' due to the third rail electrification.

We returned to Brighton station where we caught an electric train to Lewes, travelling via London Road, Moulsecoomb and Falmer.

LEWES

Steam locomotives:
30047 30049 31771 32343
32441 32467 32475 42087
80147 80152

Seven SR tanks were on shed, the other tanks noted being one LMS 2-6-4 and Standard Class '4s'. The only diesels noted were two 0-6-0 shunters. One main-line electric locomotive was noted on

steep climb we caught a brief glimpse of the locomotive depot and yard way down below us. We did not have a permit to enter the depot, but we did manage to enter without being spotted by any railway officials, which was quite surprising considering the limited means of access.

The depot had 14 roads and was a very large building of block-end design, situated in the fork of the Portsmouth and London lines. Although located close to the ter-

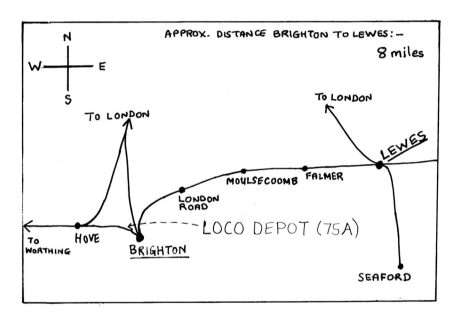

APPROX. DISTANCE BRIGHTON TO LEWES :— 8 miles

BRIGHTON DEPOT

Steam locomotives:

30053	30055	30056	30540	30544	30547	30927	31325	31487	31489	31760	31762	31776
31777	31778	31798	31890	31898	31904	32165	32166	32339	32521	32529	32646	34021
34046	34048	42080	80011	80015	80146	80149	80150	80151				

Diesel locomotives:
13012 13219

37 locomotives on shed

the forward journey, the Bulleid-designed No 20002.

We were lucky enough to see the famous electric train, the ten-carriage chocolate-and-cream-liveried 'Brighton Belle', which consisted of two five-carriage units, Nos 3051 and 3052.

The name 'Pullman' was, and still is, very much respected on our railway system as the ultimate in comfort and personal service to the rail traveller, that is if he or she requires this 1st Class service with its higher charges for its use. George Mortimer Pullman was an American and it was he that was responsible for introducing dining cars. His first cars were introduced in Canada in 1867; being known as 'hotel cars', they were converted

to sleepers at night. Pullmans were first introduced in England in 1874. At first they were pre-fabricated in the USA, then erected in England.

Unfortunately it was not possible on this visit to obtain admittance to Brighton Locomotive Works, but it was interesting to note that some of the Standard Class '4' 2-6-4 tanks seen that day had only just been built at this Works - in fact,

No 80154 (not noted) was the final engine built there and had been turned out less than a month earlier on 20 March 1957.

Repairs at the Works ceased in 1958 and some time later a small number of locomotives, made redundant by the Kent electrification scheme, were stored there for a while and this proved a source of great irritation for my friend Eddie Rooke, who, like most spotters of that day, was unaware of this hiding place and in fact needed one of their numbers to 'clear' his Southern Region numbers.

For some while after closure the Works were used for the manufacture of 'bubble cars'. They were demolished in 1969 to become a car park.

READING

SUNDAY 21 APRIL

Our departure from Portsmouth & Southsea High Level was at 10.35 am (a Wolverhampton excursion). I went on this trip with Eddie

Rooke and Terry Hunt, and the return fare was 8/6d.

We were steam-hauled by Class 'BB' ('Battle of Britain') 4-6-2 locomotive No 34063 *229 Squadron*.

On our arrival at Reading West we alighted from the excursion and proceeded to make the 10-minute walk to the Western

Region depot.

The county town of Berkshire had three railway stations, the largest being Reading General. Another important building was the Signal Works, covering about 8 acres, possibly the largest of its kind in Britain. The two engine sheds, one SR and one GWR,

---

81 D — READING DEPOT AND STATION

Steam locomotives:

1028	1407	1444	1447	2246	2251	2262	2815	2826	2852	2872	2889	3219
3723	3738	4091	4606	4609	4661	4665	4670	4673	4903	4917	4922	4938
4987	4993	5006	5007	5038	5055	5061	5065	5072	5092	5351	5368	5763
5906	5942	5945	5957	5961	5965	5996	6004	6013	6015	6018	6026	6100
6101	6103	6127	6129	6131	6149	6152	6153	6161	6162	6169	6302	6338
6366	6379	6387	6394	6627	6844	6879	6959	6976	6999	7004	7005	7007
7009	7019	7708	7788	7902	8430	9309	9404	9749	9763	9791	73012	

Diesel locomotives:
13195   13196   13268

Diesel railcars:
W12   W24   W29

96 locomotives noted

Right I often used this quiet and pollution-free bus ride from Fratton to Portsmouth & Southsea or Harbour stations to start many of our railway trips. Here is a typical scene in Portsmouth's Guildhall Square at about the date of this trip, which captures the scene as I knew it. On the right can be seen the Sussex Hotel, one of the many Thomas Owen designs to be found in the city. This lively pub saw much activity and, being close to the station, benefited from passengers alighting there. Part of Portsmouth & Southsea High Level can be seen above the trolleybus on the left.
John Kinchen

Below right A 'King' Class 4-6-0. Five of this class were noted at Reading, Nos 6004/13/15/18/26.

BETWEEN PORTSMOUTH AND READING WEST VIA BASINGSTOKE

Steam locomotives:

4926	4984	4988	6962
6989	30771	30774	34005
34010			

walk taking us about 15 minutes.

The Southern engine shed was a three-road shed, originally built in the 1850s and at one time boasting an allocation of almost 20 locomotives, but at the date of this visit its numbers had probably been at least halved. It was noted that the turntable was manually operated and the coaling facilities were quite primitive, the coal being

---

 70 E

READING (SR) DEPOT

Steam locomotives:
30277 30837 31635 31868
33038 76057 76058

Diesel locomotive:
13092

8 locomotives on shed

---

were within walking distance of each other.

This depot, set in the triangle of the lines formed by the diverging Newbury and Didcot main lines and the curve leading to the main station, was a perfect location for an engine shed and sidings. At this date 81D had about 65 engines in its allocation, the majority being 'Hall' Class 4-6-0s and 'Prairie' 2-6-2 tanks of Class '6100'. It was a straight-through shed built in 1930; a repair shop was added later.

On leaving the depot we walked to the Southern Region shed, the

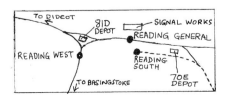

shovelled by hand. We saw Class 'N' 2-6-0 No 31868 being turned on the turntable. Trains from the South station passed this shed *en route* to Guildford and Redhill. The Western Region station, Reading General, was also visible from the yard.

We then travelled to Reading West to catch the return excursion from Wolverhampton to Portsmouth, travelling via Basingstoke, Eastleigh, Botley and Fareham.

This was my first visit to the two Reading depots. We had no permits, but both depots were successfully visited. It is of note that of the steam locomotives on shed at the Western Region depot, 18 were tank designs. The majority of the locos at this shed were in steam, and these included named main-line types such as the 'King', 'Castle', 'County', 'Hall' and 'Grange' Classes.

Of the eight engines on shed at the Southern region depot, the most interesting was 'G6' 0-6-0 tank No 30277 dating from 1894 and still in active service. I noted my last class 'S15' 4-6-0 at this depot, No 30837, to 'clear' the class; I had noted the majority of this class of 45 engines in the Portsmouth and Eastleigh areas.

NEWPORT AND PONTYPOOL

SUNDAY 28 APRIL

This trip was made by the 9.45 am excursion train from Portsmouth Harbour to Cardiff General. We purchased return tickets to Newport (High Street) station.

This was to be the first of many Sunday excursions from Portsmouth Harbour for us. I was accompanied by Eddie Rooke, David Copus, Tony Ingram ('Inky') and Terry Hunt. The return fare was 18/6d.

We were steam-hauled between Portsmouth Harbour and Salisbury by a Class 'U' 2-6-0 locomotive, but its number was not recorded. On arrival at Salisbury our engine came off and we were steam-hauled by 'Castle' 4-6-0 No 7035

BETWEEN WESTBURY AND BRISTOL VIA BATH SPA

Steam locomotives:

1004	2231	2880	2889
3177	3183	3836	3862
5002	5224	5382	6630
6827	6936	6943	6977
7312	7783	8714	70028

BETWEEN BRISTOL AND NEWPORT

Steam locomotives:

2829	4947	5050	5201
5620	6430	6847	6849
7025	7736	7918	9745
48402	90095	90403	90544

Ogmore Castle.

On our arrival at High Street station we purchased return tickets

to Griffithstown, this being the nearest station to which we could travel on a Sunday to our first depot of the visit, Pontypool Road. This depot consisted of eight roads and a roundhouse.

On leaving the depot we made the return walk to Griffithstown station where we caught a train to Newport (High Street). Our second depot of the day's visit was Newport (Ebbw Junction). We caught a double-decker bus from the city centre which took us to

A pannier tank locomotive. No fewer than 28 of these 0-6-0s were on shed at Pontypool Road. Over 1,000 were built in the 1920s and 1930s and were the mainstay of the Western Region branch-line operations.

BETWEEN SALISBURY AND WESTBURY

Steam locomotives:

1422	3840	4097	4917
4918	4945	4960	5419
5525	5911	6984	7795
7929	30674		

[Map showing railway lines around Newport. Labels: N W E S compass; GRIFFITHSTOWN; ① 86A DEPOT; ② 86B "; ③ 86G "; TO CARDIFF; TO GLOUCESTER; SEVERN TUNNEL JCN.; NEWPORT; TO BRISTOL]

86G PONTYPOOL ROAD DEPOT

Steam locomotives:

2801	2856	2872	3628	3640	3683	3685	3703	3708	3717	3779	3822	3824
3855	4119	4135	4229	4230	4592	4600	4639	4642	4668	5019	5289	5313
5388	5564	5625	5638	5659	5750	5756	5759	5775	5916	5948	6403	6424
6429	6432	6634	6636	6653	6812	6819	6828	6872	6997	7201	7206	7217
7220	7234	7235	7305	7724	7740	7796	8716	9650	9712	9730	9797	40091
48415	48417	48418	48438	48444	48460	49168	49174	49422	73021	90167	90315	

77 locomotives on shed

86 A　NEWPORT (EBBW JUNCTION) DEPOT

Steam locomotives:

1421	1509	1653	1656	2218	2280	2800	2839	2842	2858	2861	2895	2897
3103	3170	3636	3662	3691	3726	3772	3798	3800	3802	3804	3805	3827
3832	4121	4130	4168	4227	4246	4248	4271	4283	4294	4611	4916	4957
4964	4986	5014	5173	5205	5217	5227	5228	5229	5233	5238	5243	5251
5255	5256	5259	5318	5414	5649	5657	5685	5709	5732	5740	5772	5970
6102	6114	6353	6370	6401	6409	6412	6425	6439	6865	6917	6939	7020
7023	7210	7214	7218	7219	7231	7232	7233	7243	7245	7251	7253	7319
7755	7768	7771	7781	8439	8440	8453	8493	8499	8711	8766	8786	9468
9482	9662	9664	9674	9746	9778	41201	48921	90137	90179	90238	90433	90573
90676	92001	92002	92003	92005	92006	92007						

Diesel railcars:

W4	W13

126 locomotives on shed

the depot entrance; the bus displayed a 'TREDEGAR' destination.

On completing my first ever visit to this depot we left via the rear entrance and made the long walk through the allotment pathways to the next depot, Newport (Pill). This shed had tank engines only in its allocation and served part of the very large dockland area, the skyline of which was dominated by an impressive floating bridge. We eventually arrived at the depot entrance in Watch House Parade to find that the gates had been locked; this was probably because it was a Sunday and none of the engines or dockers

were working on this day. We did not have a permit to visit this depot and the only entrance was by the main gate, but this would be impossible as a gateman was in attendance. Some of us scaled the dock wall, the best part of 7 or 8 feet high, to gain entrance to the depot! I managed to make the top, from which I noted some of the tanks on shed - I and several others noted further numbers at a point some distance along the road. However, one or two of the more adventurous, including Eddie Rooke, managed to scale the wall and visit the depot, providing me with a complete list of the locomotives on shed which was, in fact,

virtually the whole allocation, since the docks were not worked on a Sunday. Not wishing to 'bull', I only counted the numbers of the ten engines I could see from the wall.

It could be seen from the top of the wall that Newport (Pill) depot was a basic lengthy two-road building, having no turntable, this layout being in complete contrast to Ebbw Junction which consisted of a double roundhouse and a 12-road workshop.

Leaving the docks area, we made the walk back to Newport (High Street) station, our route taking in the shopping areas where we made a stop for refreshments in

86 B　NEWPORT (PILL) DEPOT

Steam locomotives:

1506	1507	3652	3663	3700	4201	4214	4233	4235	4253	4258	4259	4280
4291	5200	5202	5231	5235	5250	5252	5257	5714	5733	5734	5736	5741
5747	5777	6710	6711	6725	6727	6728	6729	6730	6731	6732	6735	6739
6742	6743	6755	6756	6757	6759	6760	6764	6772	7712	7721		

50 locomotives on shed

the form of ice-creams and lollies. After this 25-minute walk we were quite exhausted and looked forward to a rest on the return train.

We picked up the return Cardiff excursion at 8.40 pm - our train was steam-hauled by the same engine used on the forward journey, No 7035 *Ogmore Castle* (this we found to be the usual practice on later excursions). Further numbers were taken on the return journey.

These were the only locomotives noted, due to darkness

NEWPORT AREA

Steam locomotives:
  3663   4091   4958   6155
  7037   70027   90529

falling. The excursion arrived back at Fratton station at approximately 1.30 am on Monday morning.

This was my first ever visit to the Newport sheds, Ebbw Junction and Pill, and my first visit to Pontypool Road. A total of 253 locomotives had been noted at these three locations; only two were diesel, both being railcars at Ebbw Junction.

The visit to Pontypool Road proved to be interesting, as the many classes noted included 'Castles', 'Halls', 'Granges', Stanier LMS 2-8-0s and '7F' 0-8-0s and numerous pannier tanks. The majority were in steam although very few were actually active when we made our visit - no fewer than 126 on shed at Newport (Ebbw Junction) speaks for itself! A very impressive sight was the six '9F'

2-10-0s, each weighing over 140 tons, simmering amidst many smaller pannier and side tank engines. We were surprised to see about seven engines in various stages of minor repair in the shed workshops.

Most helpful in locating all three locomotive depots was the *British Locomotive Shed Directory*, the property of Eddie Rooke and published by Ian Allan.

Another item of interest arose from this excursion - it was the first time that any of us had travelled through the Severn Tunnel; the longest on British Railways, it is 4 miles 628 yards long. Whilst passing through the tunnel we had the distinction of being 144 feet below sea-level - the lowest line on BR. The tunnel was constructed in 1886.

SALISBURY

SUNDAY 19 MAY

I travelled on this half-day trip to Salisbury on my own. I was steam-hauled between Fratton and Salisbury by Standard Class '4' 2-6-0 No 76010, which was shedded at Eastleigh (71A).

On arrival at Salisbury station I went to the western end of my arrival platform, from which vantage point I noted most of the locomotives listed in the table. The western end of the platform was, in fact, extremely popular with train-spotters, since move-

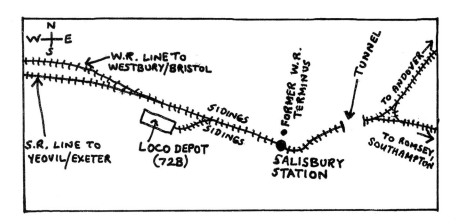

The Salisbury area. I approached from the Southampton line.

ments on and off shed could be clearly seen from this point. The depot was not visited on this occasion; without an official permit it was almost impossible to obtain admission since the narrow entrance was directly in front of the foreman's office. It was learned in later years that enthusiasts even made the long walk from the western end of the station platforms to gain admission to this ten-road straight shed!

FRATTON AND SOUTHAMPTON CENTRAL

Steam locomotives:
30455   31631   31808   31906
32646   35014   73116   76019
76064

I then caught the 7.28 pm train from Salisbury to Portsmouth. On its arrival at

SALISBURY

Steam locomotives:
  1009   3850   4945   4983
  7907   30317   30374   30449
30750   30830   30858   31804
34004   34013   34022   34044
34049   34051   34059   34108
35017   73110   73113   75078
76066

Southampton Central this train connected with the 8.26 pm from Southampton to Brighton, whose route was via St Denys, Netley, Fareham, Cosham, Havant and Chichester to Brighton. This train used the north side of the triangle, just

The ticket used: Southampton Central to Salisbury and return via Nursling and Dean. Child fare approx 2/8d.

east of Cosham station, and the locomotive was Class 'WC' ('West Country') 4-6-2 No 34037 *Callington*.

WOLVER-HAMPTON

SUNDAY 2 JUNE

This was an excursion from Portsmouth Harbour station to Wolverhampton (Low Level) to visit engine sheds to which I had not been before. The names of all the enthusiasts who accompanied me were not recorded, but the party included Eddie Rooke, David Copus and Tony Ingram ('Inky'). The return fare was 21/6d.

Departure time was at 10 am. We were steam-hauled between Portsmouth Harbour and Eastleigh by one of the Fratton allocated Class 'T9' 4-4-0s, No 30730. This engine, of a class introduced in 1899 and designed by Drummond, had seen service through two World Wars and at this date was still going strong.

Preserved locomotive No 3440 *City of Truro* was noted on passing Reading depot (81D). This was the first time I had noted this locomotive, although I was to see

READING WEST, DIDCOT AND OXFORD AREAS			
Steam locomotives:			
1420	2214	2236	2812
2872	2879	2894	3200
3210	3211	3440	3622
3738	4903	4933	4935
4942	4965	4979	5379
5697	5735	5744	5811
5960	6920	7013	7324
7329	7708	7710	8435
9640	61008	61054	73029
75025	75029	90284	

PASSING BANBURY DEPOT			
Diesel locomotives:			
13105	13106	13107	13108
13109	13110		

it on many occasions in the future when it was a regular performer on the Didcot to Southampton Terminus services.

Built at Swindon Works in 1903, a member of the 'City' Class, it had cylinders of 18 in x 26 in and driving wheels of 6 ft 8 in. On 9 May 1904 this engine made history with a speed record of over 100 mph which stood unchallenged for over 30 years. This classic run was made by the Great Western with the Ocean Mails (a purely Post Office train, carrying no passengers). Churchward-designed No 3440 ran from Plymouth to Bristol in 128 minutes. The average speed to Exeter was 55.71 mph, then Charles Rous-Marten, who was on the train, recorded a speed of 102.3 mph going down Wellington Bank!

Rough locations of the engine sheds in Wolverhampton.

BETWEEN PORTSMOUTH AND BASINGSTOKE VIA EASTLEIGH			
Steam locomotives:			
4902	30042	30763	30774
30789	31810	34012	34063
35010	35016	35018	35019
35022	41293	42094	82016

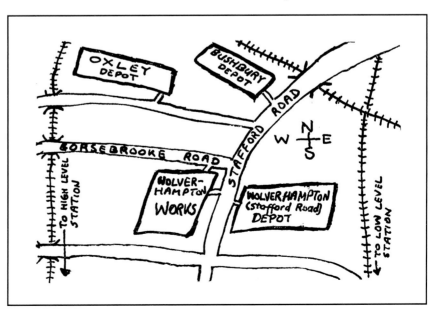

BETWEEN BANBURY AND LEAMINGTON SPA

Steam locomotives:

2804	2823	2860	2869
3624	3664	3792	3793
3847	4147	4926	4962
5045	5185	5332	5381
5929	5930	5947	6387
6810	6864	7239	7760
8109	9314	9614	44938
49304	73019	75024	90466
90716			

Diesel railcar:
W17

BIRMINGHAM AND WOLVERHAMPTON AREAS

Steam locomotives:

2830	3102	4076	4904
4964	5050	5080	5088
5180	5188	5198	6019
6859	6949	8417	8488
9498	9620	42627	

On our eventual arrival at Wolverhampton (Low Level) station at about 2.45 pm, we made the short walk to the bus stop where we caught a No 33 bus to Jones Road - this would take us near our first depot of the visit, Oxley. This particular route had, at the time of this visit, trolley buses in operation.

The depot was a large double roundhouse building with a lifting shop.

We then made the 5-minute walk to the LMS depot, Bushbury, entering via Bushbury Lane. Bushbury was a very grimy-looking straight shed consisting of eight roads. There were quite a few sidings adjacent to the shed. The atmosphere was very smoky and was possibly one of the most evil-smelling depots I had ever visited!

On leaving the depot we walked back past Oxley shed and down Stafford Road towards the city for our final depot of the visit, Wolverhampton (Stafford Road). This depot covered quite a large area. It was made up of three roundhouses and two additional straight sheds together with a lifting shop.

After leaving the depot we made the walk back to the Low Level station. Our departure on the return excursion to Portsmouth was at 7.30 pm.

The numbers listed opposite were the only ones noted, as sleep overcame us on the return journey after a very active day's travelling and walking.

The excursion arrived back at Fratton station at 1.15 am (Monday) and a brisk walk home, taking Eddie Rooke and myself less than 10 minutes, rounded off an interesting day.

Permits had been used to visit all three depots; we did not visit Wolverhampton (Stafford Road)

84B OXLEY DEPOT

Steam locomotives:

2261	2802	2819	2833	2847	2850	3813	3819	3861	4913	4966	4984	4997
5350	5390	5900	5918	5941	5958	5994	6324	6353	6610	6640	6645	6815
6859	6907	6934	6975	7759	7797	7815	8428	8449	9404	9624	9739	9752
9768	48412	73034	73035	73038	90572							

Diesel locomotives:

13034	13035	13036	13037	13038	13039	13191

52 locomotives on shed

3B BUSHBURY DEPOT

Steam locomotives:

41225	42056	42428	42429	42543	42894	42974	43090	44027	44488	44859	45015	45310
45403	45404	45555	45617	45647	45669	45688	45709	47397	47473	48674	48915	49037
49044	49167	49247	49275	58119	58183	58204						

33 locomotives on shed

WOLVERHAMPTON (STAFFORD RD) DEPOT

Steam locomotives:

1013	1453	1502	2210	3615	3649	3732	3749	3756	3769	4079	4083	4089
4094	4103	4695	4696	4990	5010	5031	5047	5106	5151	5161	5176	5179
5187	5191	5192	5312	5375	5416	5517	5541	5684	5690	5715	5763	5764
5944	5987	6001	6006	6014	6020	6022	6105	6111	6152	6160	6418	6422
6811	6848	6862	6951	6956	6964	6987	7026	7303	7430	7441	8726	8734
8752	8758	8764	9308	9428	9455	9496	9654					

73 locomotives on shed

BETWEEN WOLVERHAMPTON AND EASTLEIGH

Steam locomotives:

3102	4104	4112	4172
5166	5194	5966	6005
6106	6134	7404	30862
35005	73157		

Works as we did not have a permit. The Works appeared to be locked up, probably as it was a Sunday.

Only seven diesels were seen at the three depots, all being 0-6-0 shunters at Oxley. The 0-6-0 diesel shunters noted on passing Banbury, Nos 13105 to 13110 inclusive, had only been allocated there recently. Seven 'King' Class 4-6-0s were noted, five of these being at Stafford Road shed - noting five out of a class of 30 in one location was quite a surprise.

BRISTOL

SUNDAY 16 JUNE

This was a Portsmouth Harbour to Cardiff excursion, and departure was at 10.30 am. A group of five enthusiasts travelled and it was my first trip to the Bristol area. The return fare was 12/3d. A change of

SALISBURY TO BRISTOL

Steam locomotives:

1016	2838	3645	4096
4660	5035	5718	5974
6021	6107	6306	6977
7727	7915	41203	45577
70027	73038	73132	

locomotive was made at Salisbury.

On arrival at Stapleton Road station we walked to Bristol (Barrow Road) depot which took us about 15 minutes. This was a roundhouse-type depot with a small yard at the rear. It had quite a few sidings on one side of the building, and a footbridge spanned the yard. Official entry was via this bridge, but, as we had no permits

BRISTOL (BARROW ROAD) DEPOT

Steam locomotives:

40116	40332	40413	40426	40489	40564	41207	41208	41240	41879	43313	43427	43444
43464	43506	43593	43712	43926	44035	44045	44123	44226	44411	44424	44466	44534
44553	44563	44569	44659	44672	44805	44811	44814	44830	44841	44945	44962	45040
45186	45662	45663	45690	45699	47333	47544	47550	47552	47678	48694	51202	51212
73011	73142											

54 locomotives on shed

⬭ 82 A · BRISTOL (BATH ROAD) DEPOT

Steam locomotives:

1009	1021	1454	3623	3676	3692	3720	3759	4077	4524	4536	4567	4582
4595	4597	4647	4697	4945	4958	5019	5027	5040	5048	5057	5064	5067
5197	5525	5528	5547	5559	5561	5910	5924	5958	5992	6023	6137	6360
6601	6855	6900	6936	6945	6957	6981	7011	7015	7018	7028	7035	7300
7907	7924	8741	8744	8790	9488	41202						

Diesel railcars:
W23 W28

61 locomotives on shed

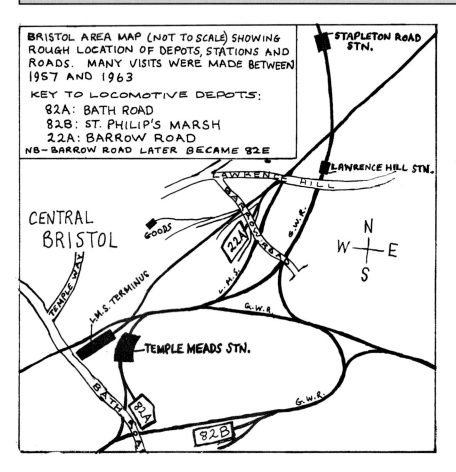

Class 'OF' 'Pug' 0-4-0 saddle tank, so nicknamed because of its shape. Introduced 1891; weight 21 tons 5 cwt; driving wheels 3 ft 0³/₈ in diameter. Two 'Pugs' were on shed at Barrow Road, Nos 51202 and 51212.

engines noted at Bath Road carried names, reflecting the depot's status as a main-line installation, with a prominent selection of large passenger types on shed. The accompanying list also includes several engines undergoing repair in the depot works.

Bath Road shed consisted of ten roads with a four-road repair shop, substantial sidings and two turntables, both overlooking the River Avon. The end of the longest platform at Temple Meads station was in close proximity to the depot and it was an ideal location for train-spotting.

On this and other trips we had often noted several diesel railcars, two of which, W23 and W28, were at Bath Road. The GWR was the first main-line railway to introduce

on this trip, entry was 'over the wall' at the rear of the shed!

On completing our visit to Barrow Road we continued our walk to the second depot of the visit, the main-line Western Region shed, Bristol (Bath Road). Our route took us through the back streets via Lawrence Hill,

Clarence Road, West Street, Old Market Street, Temple Way, Victoria Street and finally Bath Parade. Although the distance was less than one mile, the use of the *Locomotive Shed Directory* proved to be a great asset, the walk taking us over 20 minutes.

Thirty out of the 59 steam

82B ST PHILIP'S MARSH DEPOT

Steam locomotives:

1649	1669	2213	2215	2265	2269	2811	2844	2851	2863	2891	3215	3604
3632	3643	3758	3764	3765	3773	3784	3795	3800	3817	3850	4131	4262
4688	4706	4927	4951	4975	4976	5360	5642	5904	5952	5982	6308	6362
6363	6374	6391	6630	6656	6670	6671	6811	6835	6842	6846	6864	6867
6907	7231	7250	7323	7719	7728	7729	7749	7790	7795	7929	8491	8703
8714	8737	8739	8746	8747	8795	9495	9499	9601	9610	9771	46506	46525
48408	48410	48430	48434	48436	48450	48459	48461	48463	48470	48475	73019	73029
73039	90563	90676										

Diesel locomotives:

13000	13001	13002	13003	13182	13183	13184	13185	13186	13187	13255	13256	13257

107 locomotives on shed

diesel railcars, which it did on a small scale from 1934 onwards. They were single units of a stream-lined design, and some were used for parcels services.

We left 82A depot via a rear entrance and crossed a double-track railway to gain entrance to our third and final depot of the visit, St Philip's Marsh. This unofficial route took us less than 5 minutes. I recall reading a sign prohibiting 'King' Class locomotives from using these tracks.

Of the 94 steam locomotives on shed at St Philip's Marsh, only 15 were named passenger types, which suggested that, unlike Bath Road depot, this one was dominated by freight and mixed traffic designs - this included no fewer than 40 tank engines of various

deigns. The accompanying list also includes about four locomotives undergoing repairs in the two-road repair shop which adjoined the double roundhouse.

It was now early evening and we were all quite foot weary, so we decided to get some food and drink in Temple Meads station buffet and at the same time have a chance to sit down and rest.

After our refreshments we were once again back on our feet and walked back to Bristol (Stapleton Road) station to catch the return excursion from Cardiff to Portsmouth Harbour, which departed, on time, at 9.15 pm.

My first visit to the three Bristol depots produced a grand total of 207 steam engines! The highlight of our visit was Barrow Road

(22A), where all 54 on shed were steam and all were 'cops'. The sight of the two 0-4-0 saddle tanks, Nos 51202 and 51212, the Class '1F' 0-6-0 tank No 41879 and the Class '3F' 0-6-0s introduced in 1878 and 1885 respectively, will always be remembered. Apart from these ancient, but still in working order, engines, there were no fewer than 11 'Black Fives' and four 'Jubilee' 4-6-0s at this grimy, over-crowded depot.

Bath Road (82A) was impressive and well worth the visit. 'Castle' Class 4-6-0s were much in evidence.

St Philip's Marsh (82B) covered a very large area and it took us a considerable time to note every engine in the depot and yards, including the works.

HORSHAM, THREE BRIDGES, REDHILL AND CLAPHAM JUNCTION

SATURDAY 29 JUNE

We departed from Fratton station on the 6.19 am electric unit train to London (Victoria) travelling via Barnham, Arundel and Pulborough to Horsham. The return fare was 9/10d. On our arrival at Horsham station we made the 5-minute walk to the locomotive depot.

The depot was of an unusual

design, being a semi-roundhouse with the tracks leading into the partly covered depot from the turntable in the centre. This was known as an open roundhouse and was very rarely seen on my visits, the only other one in this area being at Guildford, which by this date I had not yet visited. Other depots of this design were to be found at such scattered points as Carlisle (Upperby), Middlesbrough and St Blazey in Cornwall.

HORSHAM DEPOT

Steam locomotives:
30047 30050 30051 30053
30544 30545 30547 31410
31521 32347 32463 32480
32519 32522 32527 32534
32541 32543 42101

Diesel locomotive:
D3218

20 locomotives on shed

We then travelled by electric train to the next depot of the visit, Three Bridges. We made the 5-minute walk from the station via an electricity sub-station and a cinder path to the locomotive depot entrance. The shed consisted of just three roads with a water tower incorporated into the building. A 60-foot turntable was situated alongside the shed.

After Three Bridges we returned to the station where we caught an electric unit train to Redhill. On arrival at Redhill we made the 5-minute walk via Station Road and then a private road which led us to

THREE BRIDGES DEPOT

Steam locomotives:
30052 31310 31530 32343
32344 32345 32348 32350
32450 32451 32523 32529

12 locomotives on shed

REDHILL DEPOT

Steam locomotives:
 6302 30545 31612 31617
31631 31635 31777 31786
31810 31839 31862 31866
31869 32507 32544 32560
76054 76055 76057 76060
76062 80012 80152 80153

Diesel locomotive:
13223

25 locomotives on shed

the depot gate. This three-road shed was situated in a very cramped position in an angle of the Brighton and Tonbridge lines. It had a wheel-drop and a turntable.

We returned to the station and caught another electric unit train, our destination being Clapham Junction, the largest passenger station on British Railways, covering an area of 27³/₄ acres!

Of the 24 engines noted at Clapham, six were 'Merchant Navy' Class 4-6-2s, all employed on expresses either to or from Waterloo. All the locomotives at

BETWEEN REDHILL AND CLAPHAM JUNCTION

Steam locomotives:
30041 30774 30801 30852
31487 34076 42080

CLAPHAM JUNCTION

Steam locomotives:
30043 30319 30491 30520
30770 30907 31412 31904
31907 32451 32498 34048
34065 34107 35008 35010
35016 35022 35026 35027
42068 42105 73119 76069

Class 'M7' 0-4-4 tanks Nos 30043 and 30319, introduced in 1897, were noted on empty carriage duties between Waterloo and Clapham Junction sidings. Others of this class had been noted previously at both Horsham and Three Bridges depots as well as between stations.

BETWEEN CLAPHAM JUNCTION AND FRATTON

Steam locomotives:
 5370 6379 7317 30906
31763 31778 31797 31863
31864 32470 32526 32534
32551 42068 42082 76059

Clapham Junction were noted in just 35 minutes!

We returned to Portsmouth travelling via Redhill, Three Bridges, Horsham and Arundel. Some of the SR electric unit numbers noted on this trip were: 1852, 1890, 2687, 2923, 2940, 2954, 3001, 3009, 4101, 4111, 4307, 4378, 4502, 4511, 4700 and 4736.

NOTTINGHAM

SUNDAY 28 JULY

This was an excursion to Nottingham (Victoria), the return fare being 24/9d. I went on this trip with Eddie Rooke, David Copus and 'Norman'. Norman was a middle-aged railway enthusiast, famed for his addiction to cigarettes, whom I and my friends had often met at Fratton station footbridge. He decided to join us on this excursion as he had not visited depots in Nottingham during the last 20 years. He was a much travelled enthusiast, especially on the Western Region, when, at about this date, he needed only six engines to 'clear' the region! Norman had often told us many stories of his past railway journeys and experiences whilst standing on the station footbridge at Fratton. He could easily be recognised as he always had a cigarette end in his mouth! He lived in Lake Road, Portsmouth.

The excursion departed on time at

The rough locations of stations between Portsmouth and Nottingham - approximately 175 miles. Note that Nottingham is due north of Portsmouth.

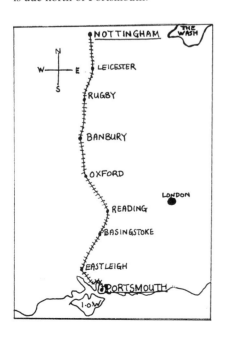

9.30 am and we were steam-hauled to Eastleigh by Fratton-allocated Class 'T9' 4-4-0 No 30732. Our train consisted of ten carriages.

PASSING FRATTON DEPOT

Steam locomotives:
30022 30356 30785 73111
76015 76068

On arrival at Eastleigh, the 'T9' was replaced by 'Lord Nelson' 4-6-0 No 30854 *Howard of Effingham*.

EASTLEIGH, WINCHESTER AND BASINGSTOKE AREAS

Steam locomotives:
5965   30120 30212 30306
30316 30488 30749 30786
30855 30859 31639 31799
31813 32342 34010 34020
34051 35007 41293 48774
48775 73083 76012 82014

Diesel locomotives:
13014 15235

LMS Class '8F' 2-8-0s Nos 48774/5 were noted on passing Eastleigh Works yard, having been overhauled after return from War Department service abroad.

On reaching Basingstoke we had our second change of locomotive; the 'Lord Nelson' came off and travelled 'light' to the nearby depot, while Western Region 'Hall' Class 4-6-0 No 5900 *Hinderton Hall* took over. This engine then hauled the excursion through to Nottingham (Victoria). Our arrival time at Nottingham was about 2 pm. We then proceeded by Trent bus service No 67 from Huntingdon Street to Victoria Road (Netherfield) to get to our first depot, Colwick. This was a

READING AREA

Steam locomotives:
2253   2867   4969   5037
6923   7788   9407   9791
70019

OXFORD AREA

Steam locomotives:
1502   2214   2236   2825
3212   3827   4649   4664
4907   4913   4993   5090
5380   5397   5943   5947
5960   6922   7238   7305
7815   8435   48369 61177
64836 80083 90284 90355

BANBURY AREA

Steam locomotives:
2246   3844   5047   5335
5361   5379   5404   5409
5930   6867   7807   7914
9653   73032

Diesel locomotive:
13106

RUGBY AND LEICESTER AREAS

Steam locomotives:
6116   61187 61368 61376
61418 61804 61974 62063
73157 90073 90507 90514
90648

massive 18-road straight shed. The coaling plant and turntable were a considerable distance from the main shed building.

Prominent classes at this freight-dominated depot were 'B1' 4-6-0s, 'K2' 2-6-0s, '01' and '04' 2-8-0 freight types, 'J69' 0-6-0s and, quite unique, the Class 'J52' saddle-tanks, Nos 68768/85, 68829/60/63/71/82/87. Also of note were the large 4-6-2 'Pacific' tanks of Class 'A5' (Nos 69800-12), each weighing over 85 tons. A total of 39 'WD' 2-8-0s (Nos

COLWICK DEPOT

Steam locomotives:

60878	61056	61066	61088	61185	61369	61380	61723	61731	61738	61739	61752	61754
61766	61780	61833	61842	61888	61914	61941	61982	63602	63614	63638	63639	63647
63657	63674	63675	63694	63699	63729	63816	63829	63839	63859	63873	64183	64195
64199	64200	64202	64213	64215	64221	64225	64230	64235	64238	64239	64248	64249
64257	64267	64273	64338	64345	64361	64384	64388	64397	64438	64712	64716	64735
64739	64741	64747	64762	64798	64823	64827	64832	64974	64983	64988	67760	67786
67788	68550	68601	68629	68768	68785	68829	68860	68863	68871	68882	68887	68893
68927	68950	68967	68975	69800	69803	69804	69805	69807	69810	69812	90000	90003
90024	90025	90038	90050	90052	90053	90075	90084	90097	90103	90115	90118	90130
90139	90153	90154	90185	90189	90202	90263	90269	90296	90303	90368	90384	90394
90432	90437	90460	90473	90496	90499	90519	90522	90629	90634	90703	92011	

142 locomotives on shed

NOTTINGHAM DEPOT

Steam locomotives:

40079	40411	40454	40461	40487	40493	40542	40553	40632	41712	42140	42185	42331
42339	42342	42361	43040	43249	43558	43729	43856	43903	43917	43918	43928	43958
43962	44010	44018	44021	44030	44033	44131	44132	44151	44158	44195	44215	44245
44313	44401	44414	44457	44555	44578	44745	44918	45088	45152	45554	46497	47277
47631	48053	48064	48108	48117	48129	48218	48260	48279	48282	48313	48337	48377
48528	48635	48639	48644	48666	48675	58137	58175	62564	73002	73067	75056	75063
92122												

Diesel locomotives:

12049	12050	12051	12097	12098	13083	13084	13085	13246	13247	13290

90 locomotives on shed

Class '1F' 0-6-0 tank No 41712 was 79 years old and still in steam. Some very old but working class '3F' 0-6-0s were also seen: Nos 43249, 43558 and 43729 (1885).

90000-90703) at one location must have been some kind of a record!

We continued by bus to our next depot, Nottingham itself, which consisted of three round-houses with a small works attached to the end of the southerly round-house. Classes seen here ranged from 'Jinty' 0-6-0 tanks to '8F' 2-8-0s, 'Black Fives', Standards and a Class '9F' 2-10-0.

A rough map of Nottingham, showing the location of the locomotive depots.

Leaving the depot, we made our way to Nottingham (Victoria) station; we had time for some food and drink before catching the return excursion to Portsmouth.

Our arrival back at Fratton station was just before 1.15 am (Monday).

NOTTINGHAM AND LEICESTER AREAS

Steam locomotives:
45690 61327 61752 64256

This was my first visit to sheds in Nottingham and we were once again aided in locating both depots by the use of the *British Locomotive Shed Directory*. We did not have permits for this visit, but nevertheless we managed to get round all right. We were approached by the foreman at Colwick who asked us for our permit - Norman immediately offered him a cigarette and casually explained to him that we had come from Portsmouth on a day excursion especially to visit this depot, and after a short conversation he told us that we could proceed but warned us that it would be at our own risk.

Nearly all the engines noted at both sheds were in steam - the majority were simmering inside the shed buildings awaiting their respective duties for the week ahead. Being a Sunday, we noted a high percentage of engines allocated to these depots, something that would not have been possible on a weekday.

All agreed that another visit be made to Nottingham, possibly taking in Toton depot.

EASTLEIGH

MONDAY 5 AUGUST

I went on this local trip alone. I was steam-hauled between Fratton and Eastleigh by Standard Class '4' 2-6-0 No 76019. The route was via Fareham and Botley and the journey took approximately 45 minutes. I noted 'King Arthur' Class 4-6-0 No 30750 *Morgan le Fay* on passing Eastleigh Works. I had planned to visit the depot, the station and Campbell Road bridge and to take some photographs.

The locomotives listed were noted during a stay of about 50 minutes.

EASTLEIGH STATION

Steam locomotives:
7905	30048	30233	30300
30738	30785	30860	31612
31619	31628	31637	34040
34106	35010	35012	35020
35022	73112	76009	76025
76027	76065	82016	

EASTLEIGH DEPOT

Steam locomotives:
2214	3206	4993	7911	30028	30029	30030	30032	30033	30082	30108	30117	30120
30125	30130	30229	30250	30283	30284	30285	30287	30288	30306	30308	30328	30375
30377	30378	30379	30476	30477	30479	30480	30486	30489	30506	30512	30522	30530
30531	30532	30543	30566	30718	30757	30772	30773	30781	30782	30786	30787	30788
30789	30834	30853	30855	30857	30861	30862	30863	31629	31802	31808	32331	32349
32424	32491	32510	32556	32557	32559	32579	33020	33021	33023	34002	34005	34008
34012	34027	34090	34109	41293	48774	76009	76010	76011	76012	76014	76015	76026
76028	76060	76067	82012	82014	82015							

Diesel locomotives:
13010	13011	13012	13013	13014	15231	15233	15234	15236

106 locomotives on shed

No 30757 was a Class '757' 0-6-2 tank of Hawthorn Leslie design for Plymouth Docks and South Western Joint Railway. Named *Earl of Mount Edgcumbe*.

No 32424 was a Class 'H2' 4-4-2 'Atlantic' of Marsh LB&SCR design. Named *Beachy Head*.

'Battle of Britain' 4-6-2 No 34090 was chosen as the engine to commemorate the Southern Railway's 25 years of existence - named *Sir Eustace Missenden, Southern Railway* after the last General Manager of the private company. No 34090 had been noted on the 'ex-Works turn' at Fratton during July.

Above Eastleigh Depot yard - Class 'N15' ('King Arthur') 4-6-0 No 30772 *Sir Percivale* in company with Drummond-designed Class 'M7' 0-4-4 tank No 30029.

Right From Campbell Road Bridge: Rebuilt 'Merchant Navy' 4-6-2 No 35020 *Bibby Line* speeds towards Southampton whilst Class 'M7' 0-4-4 tank No 30048 is employed on empty carriage duties.

BARRY AND CARDIFF

SUNDAY 18 AUGUST

This was an excursion from Portsmouth Harbour to Cardiff General, and departure time was 10 am. I went on this trip with the following local railway enthusiasts: Tony Ingram ('Inky'), Vic Coppin, 'Norman', 'Gaffer' Bleach and John 'Plymouth' Jones. Eddie Rooke travelled on the same excursion, but he, with some other enthusiasts, travelled separately and visited Llantrisant instead of Cardiff (Cathays) depot, the reason for this being that 'Norman' needed one of his last few GWR numbers, which was allocated to

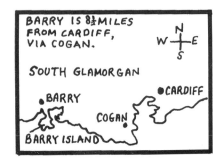

BARRY IS 8½ MILES FROM CARDIFF, VIA COGAN.

SOUTH GLAMORGAN

• BARRY   • CARDIFF

COGAN

BARRY ISLAND

this depot. The return fare was 22/6d. We were steam-hauled from Portsmouth Harbour station by 'West Country' 4-6-2 No 34010 *Sidmouth*.

We had been told previously to look out for 'Gaffer' at Portchester station. As we leaned out of the carriage window on approaching the station we immediately spotted him by virtue of him sporting a pair of luminous green socks, which were made more obvious as he was wearing tight jeans, the turn-ups of which finished well up his legs, thus showing maximum lumination!

No 34010 came off our excursion at Salisbury and 'Hall' Class 4-6-0 No 4967 *Shirenewton Hall* took over; No 4967 continued to Cardiff General where it came off and travelled 'light' to Canton depot. The same engine would be used on the return journey.

SOUTHAMPTON, ROMSEY AND SALISBURY AREAS

Steam locomotives:
2854   30067   30334   34093

WESTBURY AND BRISTOL AREAS

Steam locomotives:

1410	3795	4567	4607
4671	4932	4940	4945
4946	5038	5046	5323
5358	6163	6828	6875
6930	6957	7237	7923
9721	9745		

SEVERN TUNNEL, NEWPORT AND CARDIFF AREAS

Steam locomotives:

2231	2801	2805	2826
3172	3634	3838	4119
4161	4163	4215	4289
4611	4655	4983	5035
5078	5776	6102	6119
6330	6349	6370	6412
6430	6622	6626	6635
6643	6823	6873	6966
6971	7302	8741	9461
9494	9674	9713	9759
9778	90069	90238	

Diesel locomotives:

13102	13185	13189	13190

Although it was a Sunday, the journey through the Bristol area still proved to be of interest - engines were in sidings awaiting duties and the noting of several locomotives employed on permanent way trains added extra interest.

On arrival at Cardiff we purchased return tickets to Barry Town.

We made the walk to Barry engine shed yard via the edge of the station platform; this obviously was *not* the route given in the *Shed Directory*, but it did prove to

be 5 minutes quicker than the suggested route.

Up to this point we had noted 42 tank locomotives, the majority of these being seen on passing Severn Tunnel Junction and Newport (Ebbw Junction) engine sheds, and all the engines seen at Barry, with the exception of Class '7F' 0-8-0 No 49064, were tank designs (No 49064 had worked in on a Sunday excursion from Tredegar).

Barry depot consisted of a six-road straight shed together with a large yard and sidings on both sides of the building with an additional small yard at the rear of the shed where a turntable was also located.

Barry also had a large separate Works some distance from the depot. On this occasion we could not enter as it was locked up, but we did manage to note four locomotives through the windows.

BARRY WORKS

Steam locomotives:
4690	6714	9638	82042

BETWEEN BARRY AND CARDIFF

Steam locomotives:
4918	5084	6362	6370
6939	7252	7322	9461
9713	70020		

Returning to Barry Town station we caught a train to Cardiff General.

We then walked to the next depot of our visit, Cardiff (Canton); the walk to the shed took us 15 minutes.

Canton was a large six-road straight shed with a roundhouse and a single repair shop and numerous sidings stretching over a

BETWEEN CARDIFF AND BARRY TOWN

Steam locomotives:
4081	4097	4122	4692
5611	5613	5632	5652
5674	82043		

BARRY DEPOT

Steam locomotives:
1600	4157	4168	4177	4578	4600	4601	4610	4674	5521	5600	5609	5619
5621	5664	5667	5729	5769	6415	6427	6615	6619	6621	6637	6641	6658
6685	6712	6721	6722	6724	6733	6738	6740	6745	6746	6747	6748	6750
6753	6754	6758	6770	6771	7230	7241	8446	8450	8453	8459	8465	8766
9453	9468	9622	9631	9676	49064	82036	82037	82040	82044			

62 locomotives on shed

CARDIFF (CANTON) DEPOT

Steam locomotives:
1026	1447	1508	2805	2811	2837	2838	3176	3670	3755	3798	3809	3810
3845	4073	4137	4226	4254	4267	4297	4633	4903	4932	4964	4973	4974
4996	5062	5201	5207	5218	5334	5602	5679	5705	5749	5786	5911	5913
5970	5989	6331	6333	6352	6353	6384	6399	6644	6806	6807	6946	6949
6958	6969	7023	7775	8439	8447	8723	8728	8776	9306	9426	9427	9459
9493	9603	9648	48409	70021	70023	70024	70027	73001	75004	75007	75009	75021
75029	90125	90188	90201	90238	90524	90693	90701					

86 locomotives on shed

wide area, the majority of which could be viewed from the substantial footbridge which spanned the entire width of the complex.

We caught a bus to the entrance of our next depot, Cardiff East Dock. This depot served part of the very large dockland area in which it was situated, and was an eight-road straight shed with a single-road repair shop and turntable. The network of railways in South Wales was quite extensive at the time of this visit, but nothing like it was at the turn of the century when the Welsh Valleys were served by their own privately owned railways, such as the Taff Vale, the Rhymney Railway and the Barry Railway, together with many other smaller lines. Many of the original tank engines from these and other privately owned railways survived to enter British Railways ownership, and we noted three of these on shed at Cardiff East Dock, Nos 36, 38 and 42, all Class 'RR' (Rhymney Railway) 0-6-2

tanks. The South Wales lines were important because their main objective was the carrying of coal from the mines down to the docks at Barry, Cardiff and Newport.

Our fourth and final shed visit was Cardiff (Cathays), located about three-quarters of a mile north of Cardiff (Queen Street) station. It was quite a large five-road depot with a five-road repair bay adjoining the shed.

On completion of our visits we made our way towards Cardiff General station. At this date Cardiff still had trolleybuses of both double-deck and single-deck type - it was on one of the unique single-deck buses that we travelled between Cathays and the General station.

On the return journey I met up with Eddie Rooke in the Restaurant Car (these were invariably used on the Sunday excursions). It was interesting to compare the lists of numbers that we had each seen at different times of

the day at Barry, Canton and East Dock sheds, since there were a surprising number of variations considering that it was a Sunday. As already stated, Eddie visited Llantrisant, a shed I personally never managed to get to, but for information purposes a list is given here of the engines noted at this small three-lane shed.

Arrival time at Fratton was about 1 am (Monday).

86 D

LLANTRISANT DEPOT

Steam locomotives:

1471	3612	3617	3644
3656	3680	3776	4208
4261	4268	4620	5708
5788	9780		

14 locomotives on shed

88 B

CARDIFF EAST DOCK DEPOT

Steam locomotives:

36	38	42	3400	3401	3402	3403	3404	3405	3406	3407	3409	3681
3694	4626	4631	4686	5687	6408	6612	6701	6702	6703	6704	6705	6706
6708	6709	6736	6744	6751	6765	6767	6773	6775	8414	8416	8424	8429
8437	8438	8441	8457	9443	9473	9477	9677	9679				

Diesel locomotives:

13260	13261	13262	13263	13264	13265	13362	13363	13364	13366

58 locomotives on shed

88 A

CARDIFF (CATHAYS) DEPOT

Steam locomotives:

3641	3727	4101	4123	4124	4126	4580	4616	4672	4698	5511	5527	5534
5570	5574	5622	5630	5636	5654	5663	5670	5683	5692	6402	6434	6435
6436	6603	6606	6614	6647	6665	6682	7722	7738	7751	8736		

37 locomotives on shed

BETWEEN CARDIFF AND FRATTON

Steam locomotives:
2226	4143	4959	5344
6643	6844	8766	30452
70019	75077		

Cardiff single-decker trolleybus No 243, registration number KBO 961, on which we made our journey to Cardiff General station. Built in 1955 at the Crossley Works, Stockport, Lancs, it had seating for 40, a rear entrance, and was the last three-axle single-deck type built for service in Great Britain. KBO 961 later had a connection with the Portsmouth area in that it was acquired for preservation by the National Trolleybus Association and, *en route* to this museum, found its

way to Fareham station yard. It was eventually towed away by Scammell truck 368 BO. *Information supplied, and photograph taken in the early 1960s in Cardiff, by Alan Crockford, Fareham, Hampshire*

LONDON, SOUTHALL AND GUILDFORD

MONDAY 2 SEPTEMBER

I went on this day trip with Bill Jenkins and Jim Lawrence, both from Southsea. We purchased return tickets, price 13/8d, from Fratton to Waterloo, and our departure was on the 5.32 am 'workmens' train, timed to arrive at 7.48 am.

The 'workmens' arrived on

GUILDFORD AREA

Steam locomotives:
30027	30086	30326	31247
32505			

Diesel locomotive:
13099

WOKING, CLAPHAM JUNCTION AND WATERLOO

Steam locomotives:
30241	30518	30785	30922
31266	32506	34091	35016
73115			

time, and we began our day by catching a No 188 London Transport bus to the Old Kent Road. This took us near the entrance of Bricklayers Arms depot, and we entered via the cobbled goods yard.

This was quite a rambling depot, which was extremely time-consuming to visit as it included two straight sheds (old and new) containing eight and five roads respectively. Both sheds led onto a

65-foot turntable which also served a substantial repair shop, equipped with wheel-drop and other facilities. The repair shop contained three locomotives under repair.

We continued to the second depot of the visit, Hither Green, by bus. The depot was a single-ended building with six tracks, including a wheel-drop and a 65-foot turntable.

We travelled by train from Hither Green to the next depot, Norwood Junction.

BETWEEN HITHER GREEN AND NORWOOD JUNCTION

Steam locomotives:
30517	30699	30929	31851
32552	32565	33015	34083
68971	80014		

Norwood Junction was a fairly small depot, having five roads. It was constructed in pre-cast concrete and also included asbestos in its building. It had a 65-foot turntable at the rear.

Map: N W E S — WILLESDEN, OLD OAK COMMON, SOUTHALL, RIVER THAMES, Waterloo station, BRICKLAYERS ARMS, FELTHAM, STEWARTS LANE, HITHER GREEN, NORWOOD JUNCTION, GUILDFORD

BRICKLAYERS ARMS DEPOT

Steam locomotives:
30916 30918 30926 30927 30931 30932 30933 30937 30938 30939 31169 31306 31497
31533 31717 31735 31739 31817 31827 31828 31829 31851 31871 31890 31891 31899
31917 32104 32107 32408 32410 32471 32473 32538 32539 32544 32564 33017 34074
34079 34081 41300 41301 42080 75065 75066

Diesel locomotive:
15217

47 locomotives on shed

HITHER GREEN DEPOT

Steam locomotives:
30806 31018 31033 31067 31102 31287 31683 31686 31688 31689 31692 31694 31720
31724 31822 31823 31855 31857 31877 31911 31912 31916 31922 31923 31924 31925
65506 65540

Diesel locomotives:
11223 11224 11225 13273 D3460 D3467 D3469 D3470 15216 15220 15226 15229

40 locomotives on shed

NORWOOD JUNCTION DEPOT

Steam locomotives:
30533 30537 31267 31719 31827 31918 32411 32413 32414 32416 32417 32418 32447
32466 32543 32545 42104

Diesel locomotives:
11001 13049 13223 D3464 15203

22 locomotives on shed

No 11001 was a diesel-mechanical 0-6-0 type, introduced 1950. It was a Bulleid design for shunting.

Leaving the depot, we travelled by electric unit train to Queens Road, Battersea, the nearest station to our fourth depot of the visit, Stewarts Lane.

The use once again of the *British Locomotive Shed Directory* helped us to locate the shed, which was a 5-minute walk via Queenstown Road and Silverthorne Road. Stewarts Lane was a 16-road shed which was

BETWEEN NORWOOD JUNC AND QUEENS RD

Steam locomotives:
30797 30865 30918 31717
32539 34018 34097 80148

Diesel locomotives:
15212 15227

just visible from the Portsmouth-Waterloo line. It had a turntable at the far end of the yard.

Up to this point, we had noted no fewer than five Eastern Region locomotives, these being employed on transfer freight trains from the north London suburbs to the spacious sidings at Hither Green and possibly other locations in south London. Their numbers were 65506

STEWARTS LANE DEPOT

Steam locomotives:

30768	30794	30795	30908	30909	30915	31019	31265	31408	31411	31412	31504	31540
31545	31550	31551	31552	31557	31558	31576	31578	31579	31581	31582	31584	31693
31755	31789	31811	31898	31901	31905	31907	31908	32100	32102	32103	32455	34066
34070	34085	34088	34096	34103	35001	41292	42090	42096	42106	44530	68966	68987
70004	70014	73088										

55 locomotives on shed

and 65540 on shed at Hither Green, 68971 at Hither Green sidings and 68966 with 68987 on shed at Stewarts Lane.

We continued our visits, again travelling by train, departing from Queens Road, Battersea, at noon, our destination being Feltham, via Clapham Junction.

On arrival at Feltham station we made the long walk to the engine shed, this taking us nearly 25 minutes. In the vicinity of this shed were extensive marshalling yards, where the sorting of many wagons into trains bound for various destinations took place. A 'hump' was used, basically an incline over which a shunting engine pushed wagons and from which the wagons travelled on their own into the rele-

QUEENS ROAD TO FELTHAM

Steam locomotives:
30244 30488 30696 32486
33038 34022

Pullman named carriages: 'Aquila', 'Carina', 'Hawthorn', 'Medusa', 'Orion', 'Ruby' and 'Topaz'.

vant sidings. A railwayman would apply brakes to avoid collisions.

Feltham was a six-road straight shed with an adjoining repair shop. A very distinctive coaling plant dominated the scene.

On leaving the depot we walked

back to the station. We travelled by bus from near Feltham station to our sixth depot visit, Southall. This depot was situated in the fork of the main line and Brentford lines at the east end of Southall station; we gained access to the yard via a large footbridge.

This brick-built six-road shed had primarily freight engines and suburban tanks in its allocation. The shed also had a repair shop and a turntable, which was located at the rear of the building.

On leaving the depot we made our way towards London, travelling by double-decker bus to our seventh depot of the visit, Willesden. This lengthy bus ride afforded us time to consume our lunch which we had brought with us from Portsmouth.

FELTHAM DEPOT

Steam locomotives:

30038	30043	30179	30243	30339	30355	30453	30457	30492	30493	30494	30496	30499
30500	30504	30505	30508	30510	30511	30513	30517	30518	30519	30568	30687	30688
30833	30834	30839	33006	33007	33008	33010	33011	33013	33016	33018	48062	

Diesel locomotives:
13040 13041 D3042 13094 13270

43 locomotives on shed

No 30568 was a Class '0395' 0-6-0, introduced 1881 to an Adams design. At this date it was 76 years old and still in working order!

No 30688 was a Class '700' 0-6-0, introduced 1897; it had recently been involved in a head-on collision with an electric suburban unit train at Staines station, and was at Feltham awaiting being towed to works for repair.

SOUTHALL DEPOT

Steam locomotives:

1406	1426	1446	1474	1501	2205	2868	3618	3704	3800	3814	4097	4673
4944	4978	4994	5037	5042	5053	5086	5410	5727	5799	5918	5942	5953
5976	5979	5996	6002	6108	6109	6122	6126	6127	6128	6140	6147	6148
6150	6156	6157	6165	6169	6313	6360	6369	6654	6655	6816	6843	7007
7730	7910	8413	8752	8774	9305	9413	9417	9479	9701	9726	70018	90040
90152	90174	90313	90355	90365	90520	90529	90685					

Diesel locomotive:
13030

Diesel railcar:
W27

75 locomotives on shed

Nearly all the trips involved 'self-supplied' food, this being mainly sandwiches, rolls, crisps and a bottle of diluted squash. Other items such as biros, permits and a plastic mac (prior to the coming of the anorak) were always taken with us; these, in my case, were carried in a home-made haversack made by my mother - this haversack was to see many years of use and wear, having originally been used to keep potatoes in!

Willesden had a 12-road shed, a

Class 6100 2-6-2 'Prairie' tank locomotive, of which we saw 14 at Southall shed.

WILLESDEN DEPOT

Steam locomotives:

40006	40007	40016	40042	40044	40045	40046	40047	40051	40053	40064	42117	42747
42779	42812	42870	42885	42926	42966	42972	42979	43405	44116	44370	44372	44397
44440	44451	44681	44686	44742	44760	44771	45020	45027	45032	45089	45091	45096
45289	45312	45324	45350	45353	45381	45397	45404	45511	45517	45583	45603	45740
46138	46211	46230	47164	47342	47355	47361	47397	47412	47474	47505	47520	47531
47558	47675	47676	48117	48129	48154	48269	48290	48343	48600	48603	48608	48615
48624	48628	48629	48630	48649	48656	48729	48769	49070	49139	49180	49344	75036
80084	90288	92100										

Diesel locomotives:
12074   13015   13016   13017

98 locomotives on shed

OLD OAK COMMON DEPOT

81 A

Steam locomotives:

1500	2246	2816	2846	3644	3648	3688	3844	4077	4608	4700	4701	4703
4706	4902	4951	4959	4963	4965	4968	4975	4977	4982	5006	5008	5029
5034	5040	5053	5066	5067	5074	5084	5087	5093	5099	5758	5931	5940
5951	5999	6008	6013	6018	6021	6022	6024	6025	6026	6120	6121	6132
6135	6141	6142	6149	6306	6664	6838	6846	6861	6928	6950	6957	6962
6970	6973	7000	7004	7017	7024	7032	7035	7808	7903	7904	8751	8754
8756	8760	8764	8765	8768	9419	9700	9702	9703	9704	9705	9708	9709
9710	9758	9784	48450	70023	73001							

Diesel locomotive:
13032

98 locomotives on shed

roundhouse and a small works.

We then made the 5-minute walk to Old Oak Common depot, the main Western Region depot in London - this was probably the shortest distance between any two sheds in London.

Old Oak Common boasted no fewer than four roundhouses and a repair works, which was conspicuous by the fact that it had 12 roads and was serviced by a traverser.

We then walked to Willesden Junction station, catching a train to Euston.

We then caught a tube train to Waterloo, where we caught a

BETWEEN WILLESDEN JUNCTION AND EUSTON

Steam locomotives:

40125	44715	45307	45354
45380	45545	45578	45592
46147	46150	46162	46163
46226	46242	46252	46431
47522	47527	47667	80043

WATERLOO STATION AND AREA

Steam locomotives:

30133	30241	30248	30320
30322	34090	73118	73119

Portsmouth line train to Guildford, for our ninth and final visit of the day. After a very energetic day's travelling around the London area we were now quite tired!

Guildford depot, as has already been mentioned, was a curious combination of a semi-circle of separate bays, together with a four-road straight shed, engines gaining access from a turntable.

On this, my first visit to Guildford, I 'cleared' the complete allocation of locomotives.

On the way home to Fratton I briefly compared my list of engine numbers for the day with Bill Jenkins and Jim Lawrence. All nine depots were visited for the first time. In comparing

GUILDFORD DEPOT

70 C

Steam locomotives:

30026	30086	30110	30124
30238	30325	30326	30346
30349	30575	30693	30698
30705	31145	31622	31624
31625	31627	31630	31722
31800	32487	32506	33002
33003	33005	33022	33025
33026			

Diesel locomotives:
13096 13099

steam/diesel ratios at the nine depots visited, we found that we had noted 477 steam and 32 diesels (one of the latter being a railcar).

We did agree that London depots each had their own atmosphere and steam engines ruled supreme - another visit would be made.

GLOUCESTER AND CHELTENHAM

SUNDAY 1 DECEMBER

This Sunday excursion from Portsmouth Harbour to Cheltenham was my first visit to this area. The enthusiasts who accompanied me were Eddie Rooke, David Copus, Terry Hunt and David Bodenham, and the return fare was 16/3d. Our train departed at 10.12 am and we were steam-hauled by Fratton-allocated Class 'U' 2-6-0 locomotive No 31808.

BETWEEN FRATTON AND EASTLEIGH

Steam locomotives:
30030	31638	34049	35012
35017	75070	82016	

On our arrival at Eastleigh we had a change of locomotive. No 31808 was taken off and we were then steam-hauled by 'West Country' Class 4-6-2 No 34040 *Crewkerne*. Our route was via Chandlers Ford and Romsey to Salisbury, where on arrival No 34040 was taken off and we were then steam-hauled by Western Region 'County' Class 4-6-0 No 1028 *County of Warwick*. This was the first time that I had been hauled by a 'County' Class engine.

It may be worthy of note that, between Portsmouth and Salisbury, we saw 'Hampshire' diesel units 1103/09/12/15/17.

On our arrival at Bristol (Temple Meads) station, our excursion had its fourth and final change of locomotive; the 'County' was taken off and we were then steam-hauled by

SALISBURY, WESTBURY AND BRISTOL AREAS

Steam locomotives:
3676	4086	4923	4963
5076	5323	5419	5919
6325	6860	6994	7014
7794	30335	43926	44135
44534	45562	48461	73012

Diesel locomotive:
13003

Diesel railcars:
W24   W25

The railcars were noted on passing Bristol (St Philip's Marsh) depot yard.

BRISTOL AREA

Steam locomotives:
40116	41879	42766	43712
44209	44264	44321	44536
44537	45260	47552	73054
92137	92155		

No 41879 was a Class '1F' 0-6-0 tank, introduced 1878 and rebuilt with Belpaire firebox. No 43712 was a Class '3F' 0-6-0, introduced 1885 to a Johnson Midland design. Both of these locomotives were in working order, being at this date 79 and 72 years old respectively!

BETWEEN BRISTOL AND CHELTENHAM VIA GLOUCESTER

Steam locomotives:
3850	4139	4358	5514
5945	5946	6985	7810
43853	44160	44179	44567
47417			

London Midland Region Class '5' ('Black Five') 4-6-0 No 44919 on the final stage between Bristol and Cheltenham. Our train was assisted up the gradient out of Bristol by a 'banker' at the rear - No 43926, a Class '4F' 0-6-0 allocated to Barrow Road shed. We had now

been hauled by locomotives from three regions, Southern, Western and Midland!

When we arrived at Cheltenham we found that the station was unmanned. Our carriages had stopped short of the platform, so we decided to jump down on to the permanent way to alight from the excursion.

We walked from Cheltenham Spa station via Malvern Road to the engine shed, and used the cinder path leading to the depot. Cheltenham was a sub-depot of Gloucester, and was also known as Cheltenham (Malvern Road) - it was a neatly built four-road brick shed, located adjacent to Malvern Road station.

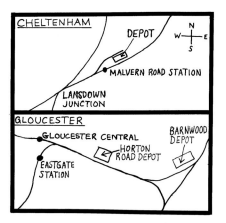

CHELTENHAM DEPOT

Steam locomotives:
3810	3824	4100	4564
5165	5182	5421	6330
6341	8488	47539	90691

Diesel railcar:
W19

13 locomotives on shed

On leaving the depot we travelled by double-decker bus to Gloucester to visit the depots there.

The first was Gloucester (Horton Road) depot, comprising a

GLOUCESTER (HORTON ROAD) DEPOT

Steam locomotives:

1424	1428	1441	1464	1605	1616	1642	2248	2254	2813	2854	3203	3809
4139	4141	4358	4573	4627	4664	5017	5018	5094	5105	5157	5530	5651
5946	6365	6394	6669	6690	6985	7006	8487	8717	8727	9438	9441	9445
9464	9471	9492	73017	90214	90573	90685						

46 locomotives on shed

GLOUCESTER (BARNWOOD) DEPOT

Steam locomotives:

40443	40489	40540	41049	41095	41535	41537	41900	42313	43258	43337	43359	43520
43754	43853	43911	43989	44035	44045	44108	44123	44179	44201	44272	44583	44811
44888	47417	47422	47506	47623	48271	48351						

33 locomotives on shed

four-road and a six-road shed, with an adjoining wheel-drop shop. There was a turntable in the yard.

We then walked to the third depot of our visit, the LMR depot at Gloucester (Barnwood). This was a single roundhouse of traditional Midland Railway design.

We then walked to the station, where we picked up the return excursion to Portsmouth which had departed from Cheltenham at about 6.30 pm. The route was once again via Bristol and Salisbury. Very few locomotives were recorded on the way home due to the darkness.

Our arrival at Fratton was at about 1 am (Monday). It had been a cold but sunny day.

BETWEEN GLOUCESTER AND BRISTOL

Steam locomotives:

5182	5418	6919	6936
44160	44567	48338	

ADDITIONAL HIGHLIGHTS OF 1957

SWINDON: 4 SEPTEMBER - Taff Vale tanks Nos 304, 346, 373, 383, 384 and 398 in for scrap, together with 'Dukedog' No 9026. Diesels under construction: Nos D800, D801 and D802; also shunters Nos 11187 to 11194 (inclusive).

BRISTOL: 6 SEPTEMBER - As we came out of St Philip's Marsh shed we noted 0-6-0 diesel shunter No 13000. We asked the driver if we could 'cab' it; he let us do this, then took us for a short ride in the yard. At Temple Meads station No 45660 *Rooke* was seen for the first time, but missed by Eddie Rooke on this occasion, as he was in the gents at the time! Surprisingly, this was an engine that eluded my good friend Eddie for many years, much to his disgust!

SWINDON: 3 NOVEMBER - We were steam-hauled between Andover Junction and Swindon Junction by Standard Class '3' 2-6-2 tank No 82039, ex-Works from Swindon. Sent to Swindon for scrapping were Rhymney tanks Nos 36, 38 and 42, Taff Vale tank No 390, 'ROD' 2-8-0 No 3016, 2-6-2 tanks Nos 3100, 3101, 3150, 3172, 3177, 3180 and 3183, and 'Dukedogs' Nos 9025 and 9028. Also noted: 'Star' 4-6-0 No 4056 *Princess Margaret*.

The Stock Shed was visited for the first time and contained Nos 2516, 2877 and 4003 *Lode Star* (the first and last of these three later being preserved in Swindon Museum). Of course the sad side of Swindon was the scrapyard, and this large area took us over 90 minutes to complete. A small covered shed, depot/works, at the very far end of the scrapyard acted as a point where spare parts, cannibalised from scrapped locomotives, were stored to be used to repair other locomotives that were fortunate enough to survive a visit to the main workshop. Sometimes a withdrawn engine would be cut up within a week of its arrival, while others would linger in the sidings for weeks, months or even longer, before eventually being cut up for scrap.

At the date of this visit some steam locomotives in the scrapyard still carried their number and nameplates, their connecting rods and some even their shedplates; some had considerable amounts of coal still in their tenders and bunkers.

THE PORTSMOUTH AREA DURING 1957

FRATTON DEPOT

Steam locomotives:

4912	4935	4987	4994	5933	6848	30130	30300	30304	30378	30456	30475	30707
30721	30729	30730	30732	30787	30788	31613	31629	31637	31638	31801	31807	31809
31890	32479	32509	32650	32694	34005	34019	34051	34056	73111	73113	73118	75075
76005	76008	76009	76012	76014	76028	76063						

46 locomotives on shed

FRATTON: SUNDAY 21 JULY - My local engine shed was visited for the first time. About ten locomotives were also noted at Fratton station, but all these would have at some time during the day been on shed.

The list of engines shown above was typical of a visit to Fratton shed and station in the late 1950s, especially on a Sunday, as this was the day that a selection of Western Region locomotives could be noted employed on excursion trains to Portsmouth Harbour station, coming from such points as Bristol, Oxford, Gloucester and Wolverhampton. On this visit I noted five 'Hall' 4-6-0s and one 'Grange' 4-6-0, all being employed on excursion trains. Of the 29 Southern Region steam locomotives noted, seven were main-line types, including 'King Arthur', 'West Country' and 'Battle of Britain' classes - it was most likely that the latter were employed on excursions.

Fratton-allocated locomotives were as follows: Nos 30729, 30730 and 30732 ('T9' 4-4-0s), 31637, 31638, 31807 and 31809 ('U' 2-6-0s), 32479 and 32509 ('E4' 0-6-2 tanks), 32650 ('A1X' 0-6-0 tank) and 32694 ('E1' 0-6-0 tank). It was unusual to note seven 'T9s' at Fratton in one day - apart from the three Fratton-allocated engines mentioned above, also noted were Nos 30300, 30304, 30707 and 30721, the latter being an Exmouth Junction (72A) allocation.

An unusual sight was 'T9s' Nos 30707 and 30732 double heading the Cardiff General train out of Fratton station. Another long-lived class noted were the 'M7' 0-4-4 tanks, Nos 30130 and 30378, introduced in 1903 and still very much in use. Finally, 11 Standard types were noted, with the Class '4' 2-6-0s being very common at Fratton as these were used to haul local trains, although Fratton did not have any Standards in its allocation. No diesels were noted, but it was likely that several 0-6-0 shunters were busy in the carriage sidings. These would be Eastleigh-allocated locomotives.

Western Region 'Grange' Class 4-6-0. One of this class, No 6848 *Toddington Grange*, was employed on an excursion; the 'Granges', together with 'Hall' Class 4-6-0s, were common visitors to Fratton.

Class 'T9' 4-4-0 No 30117 at Fratton station in the summer of 1957. *Jack Stillwell*

FRATTON: MONDAY 22 JULY - An unusual visitor to Fratton shed was 'Lord Nelson' 4-6-0 No 30856 *Lord St Vincent*.

FRATTON: JULY TO DECEMBER - I am including at this point some local railway information together with some of the engines noted in the area between 2 July and 21 December.

SATURDAY 10 AUGUST - Western Region engines noted: Nos 5947, 6325, 6831, 6878, 6922 and 6968.

SATURDAY 21 SEPTEMBER - 'Grange' 4-6-0 No 6851 *Hurst Grange* brought in a Nottingham Forest football special.

SUNDAY 13 OCTOBER - A visit was made to the depot - 28 steam locomotives and one diesel shunter were on shed. I 'cabbed'

Class 'U' 2-6-0 No 31808. Five 'Terriers' were noted, Nos 32640, 32646, 32650, 32661 and 32677. It is of note that a Class 'N' 2-6-0 from the Eastern Section always worked into Portsmouth on Sundays - on this date No 31409 from Ashford was noted.

SATURDAY 19 OCTOBER - A rare visitor was Class 'G6' 0-6-0 tank No 30274 from Templecombe depot (71H).

SATURDAY 21 DECEMBER - Another rare class at Fratton, employed on a Christmas parcels train, was Norwood Junction-allocated Class 'E4X' 0-6-2 tank No 32466.

1957 saw the introduction of 'Hampshire Diesels' - two-carriage, green-liveried units. This was the first sign of modernisation and the eventual replacement of steam

power on local trains such as the Southampton and Eastleigh services. There were 22 units, Nos 1101 to 1122, and the locals gave them the nickname of 'Wafflebugs'.

FRATTON, COSHAM, HILSEA: SATURDAY 3 AUGUST - My visit to Fratton station footbridge was broken for lunch, then in the afternoon I caught a train to Cosham for a brief visit. Leaving Cosham by trolleybus, I travelled the short distance, less than a mile, to Hilsea where I alighted and visited the site of the Hilsea Miniature Railway. I then continued by bus to Copnor Road from where I walked to Moneyfields footbridge to take photographs. The locomotive numbers listed overleaf were noted at both Fratton, Cosham and on the line between these two stations.

THE '7.06 PM'

An ex-Works steam locomotive which had been overhauled at Eastleigh Works was used between Portsmouth and Winchester City, travelling via Botley, on Mondays to Fridays, or as and when an engine was available. This locomotive would run on a parcels train which passed through Fratton station at 7.06 pm on a 'running-in' turn, prior to its return to its depot of allocation. This table shows some of the locomotives that were used on this turn during 1957.

Date	Engine	Name	Class	Allocated
July				
Tue 2nd	30792	*Sir Hervis de Revel*	'N15'	Bricklayers Arms
Wed 3rd	30771	*Sir Sagramore*	'N15'	Basingstoke
Thur 4th	"	"	"	"
Fri 5th	34046	*Braunton*	'WC'	Brighton
Mon 8th	34090	*Sir Eustace Missenden Southern Railway*	'BB'	Bricklayers Arms
Tue 9th	"	"	"	"
Wed 10th	"	"	"	"
Thur 11th	"	"	"	"
Fri 12th	30454	*Queen Guinevere*	'N15'	Salisbury
Mon 15th	34062	*17 Squadron*	'BB'	Exmouth Jcn
Tue 16th	30476	-	'H15'	Eastleigh
Thur 18th	30455	*Sir Launcelot*	'N15'	Nine Elms
Fri 19th	"	"	"	"
Mon 22nd	76068	-	'4'	Eastleigh
Tue 23rd	30784	*Sir Nerovens*	'N15'	"
Thur 25th	30790	*Sir Villiars*	'N15'	"
Fri 26th	"	"	"	"
Wed 31st	34091	*Weymouth*	'WC'	Bricklayers Arms
August				
Thur 1st	"	"	"	"
Tue 6th	30850	*Lord Nelson*	'LN'	Eastleigh
Wed 7th	30772	*Sir Percivale*	'N15'	(not noted)
Thur 8th	34041	*Wilton*	'WC'	"
September				
Fri 13th	30711	-	'T9'	Exmouth Jcn

FRATTON AND COSHAM

Steam locomotives:
5947	6831	6920	7906
30285	30301	30357	30376
30511	30732	31638	31796
31804	31808	31809	32139
32337	32509	32650	32661
32694	34016	34048	34055
75075	75079	76008	76010
76015	76025	76027	76066
76069	80154	82014	

Diesel locomotive:
13011

Above 'Hall' Class 4-6-0 No 5993 *Kirby Hall* at Cosham station on the Reading train from Portsmouth, photographed in the summer of 1957. The footbridge of 1890 vintage was built by Joseph Westwood, London. *Jack Stillwell*

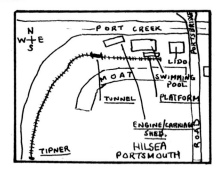

Above The Hilsea Miniature Railway. I recall as a boy travelling on the 10¼ in gauge single line, a round trip of about 1 mile. The line was discontinued in the early 1950s. The locomotive was based on ER Class 'A2/1' 4-6-2 (BR locomotive introduced 1944, miniature version 1947) built by David Curwen Ltd of Baydon, Marlborough, Wilts. Length 14 ft; weight 2½ tons; colour, apple green; named *Robin Hood*.

FRATTON AND BRIGHTON: 5 OCTOBER

The Fratton roundhouse was under repair and as a result there was the most unusual sight of no fewer than 31 locomotives all in the depot yard in front of the roundhouse.

That afternoon Brighton was visited and the opportunity was taken to visit the Volk's Electric Railway on the seafront for the first time. It was first opened in experimental form in August 1883 on a 2-foot gauge by Magnus Volk (1851-1937), and has the distinc-

Above Drummond-designed Class 'T9' 4-4-0 No 30285 (introduced in 1899) passes the familiar landmark of Hilsea Gas Works, Portsmouth. This 'T9' was allocated to Eastleigh (71A) and often visited Portsmouth with many others of the same class, nicknamed 'Greyhounds' for obvious reasons. No 30285 was working a local Southampton-Portsmouth train.

The gas works occupies approximately 40 acres on the down side of the main line, just south of Hilsea Halt (now Hilsea). There are two gas holders and many buildings. Green Lanes Crossing at this location had a large signal box near which was located a weighbridge. A 'U'-shaped track ran round most of the gas works, with a further four sidings leading off into the main works; there were also lines leading off these together with four main sidings adjacent to the main BR lines.

tion of being the first electric railway in Britain. The track runs for approximately 1¼ miles, from Aquarium to Black Rock, and is operated by Brighton Corporation.

Magnus Volk was a pioneer of electrical engineering - his house was the first in Brighton to have electric lighting. This electrified line is a very popular attraction for

STEAM ON SHED AT FRATTON, SUNDAY 29 SEPTEMBER 1957

Eddie Rooke accompanied me on this visit to Fratton locomotive depot. It was unusual for him to bring along his camera, a Brownie 127.

One of my favourite photographs is this late 1950s view capturing the true atmosphere of Fratton shed yard. I produced a pencil and colour drawing of this scene. Steam locomotives, left to right, are: Class 'E1' 0-6-0 tank No 32139, Class 'M7' 0-4-4 tank No 30376, Standard Class '4' 2-6-0 No 76014 and Class 'Q1' 0-6-0 No 33028. All four locomotives are in steam, simmering in the autumn sun awaiting their respective duties. There is only one Fratton-allocated locomotive in this group, 'E1' 0-6-0 tank No 32139, which at this date was 83 years old, having been introduced in 1874.

Fratton depot had three Class 'C2X' 0-6-0s in its allocation, Nos 32548, 32549 and 32550. No 32548 was photographed undergoing some minor repairs on the depot crane. Note the double domes. The 'C2Xs' were used mainly for carriage work between Fratton sidings and Portsmouth Harbour station, although occasionally they could be seen employed on pick-up freight trains between Fratton sidings and Chichester.

A close-up view of Class 'M7' 0-4-4 tank No 30376, allocated to Eastleigh depot. The author poses by the cab, camera in hand, ready for the next picture.

holidaymakers, giving much pleasure to both adults and children. At the date of this visit the gauge was 2 ft 8 in, and the line had been opened for 74 years (except for closure between 1940 and 1948, due to the threat of German invasion).

FRATTON: 25 DECEMBER - The depot was visited on Christmas Day, and the following steam engines were noted: Nos 30022, 30023, 30039, 30328, 30357, 30729, 30732, 31613, 31637, 31638, 31804, 31805, 31807, 32139, 32337, 32349, 32351, 32438, 32479, 32495,

32509, 32548, 32549, 32550, 32640, 32650, 32661, 32677, 32694, 73111, 76005, 76009, 76010 and 76028. Diesels: 13014 and 15233.

This, my final visit of the year to Fratton shed, in which I saw nearly all the Fratton-allocated engines on shed, proved to be another typical visit. No fewer than five Class 'M7' 0-4-4 tanks were noted; one, No 30023, was ex-Works from Eastleigh. Class 'E1' 0-6-0 tanks Nos 32139 and 32694 were at this date 83 years old, and in daily use on the Dockyard goods!

Other locomotives seen were two 'T9' 4-4-0s, six 'U' Class 2-6-0s, two Billinton-designed 'K' Class 2-6-0s, all three of the Class 'C2X' 0-6-0s (Nos 32548, 32549 and 32550) and four 'A1X' 0-6-0 tanks, used on the Hayling Island branch. Finally, a Standard Class '5' 4-6-0 and four Standard Class '4' 2-6-0s were noted.

Fratton was a roundhouse-type shed with a 50-foot turntable and it had a completely covered roof - in this it was unique on the SR. The depot was jointly shared in pre-Grouping days by the LSWR and the LB&SCR.

DOWNTOWN MEMORIES: PORTSMOUTH AND SOUTHSEA IN THE '50s

Numerous visits were made in the late 1950s to Portsmouth & Southsea station to visit the nearby Commercial Road, the city's main shopping area. Local railway enthusiasts often kept together, even when we were not visiting railway installations. Some of our favourite haunts 'downtown' were

the LDB (Landport Drapery Bazaar) on the corner of Arundel Street and Commercial Road, where a pop group would play on Saturday mornings.

Perhaps our favourite place was the ice-cream/coffee bar of Verrecchia's in the Guildhall Square. Their speciality was 'Knickerbocker Glories', which we sampled on many occasions. The interior had hard seating facing each other with a table-top separating each section. There was some very ornate glasswork which blended in well with the 1950s surroundings (a sample of this ornate interior is now preserved in

Portsmouth City Museum). The waiter was a tall man with very scruffy whiskers - we gave him the nickname 'The Wild Man from Borneo'. We would sit for an hour with one drink and he would keep coming round to our table to see if we had finished - on leaving we would tip him one halfpenny!

Another cafe frequented was opposite the Theatre Royal, and here we met up with 'Norman', one of the older railway enthusiasts. We would sit in this cafe and drink tea or coffee while at the same time observing trains crossing the high level at Portsmouth & Southsea station.

READING, SLOUGH AND BASINGSTOKE

SUNDAY 6 APRIL

Our departure from Portsmouth Harbour station was at 10.12 am - it was a Wolverhampton excursion and the return fare was 13s. We were steam-hauled by Class 'T9' 4-4-0 No 30732 (70F) to Eastleigh travelling via Fareham.

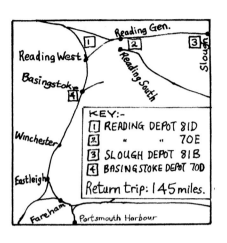

KEY:-
1. READING DEPOT 81D
2. " " 70E
3. SLOUGH DEPOT 81B
4. BASINGSTOKE DEPOT 70D

Return trip: 145 miles.

Class 'H15' 4-6-0 No 30487 and Class '0395' 0-6-0 No 30568 were noted in the scrapyard on passing Eastleigh.

"TURF" CIGARETTES
"Hall" Class 4-6-0
50 BRITISH RAILWAY LOCOMOTIVES No.16

FRATTON AND EASTLEIGH AREAS

Steam locomotives:
30032 30357 30379 30487
30495 30568 30858 34065
34070 34102 35014 73115
82014

BETWEEN EASTLEIGH AND BASINGSTOKE

Steam locomotives:
6934 6973 30456 30491
30515 34049 35026 75076
75079

Diesel locomotive:
15232

The 'T9' came off at Eastleigh and 'West Country' 4-6-2 No 34041 *Wilton* took over.

On passing Micheldever sidings we noted SR electric unit No 4506.

A further change of engine was made at Basingstoke. We were then steam-hauled to Reading

Always a common sight at Reading (81D) were members of the 'Hall' Class, one of which nearly always worked the summer service Reading General to Portsmouth train. On numerous occasions it was No 4995 *Easton Hall*.

81D   READING (WR) DEPOT

Steam locomotives:

1444	1447	2245	2262	2808	2824	2896	3219	3738	3839	3849	4078	4085
4609	4665	4670	4951	4960	4961	4962	4963	4969	4989	4995	4998	5315
5368	5763	5901	5910	5957	5973	5980	6026	6100	6101	6104	6117	6123
6126	6130	6145	6153	6302	6320	6324	6353	6843	6879	6936	6960	6968
7301	7308	7788	7906	7919	8430	9402	9403	9749	9763	9791		

Diesel locomotives:
13195 13196 13268 13269

Diesel railcars:
W33 W38

69 locomotives on shed

West by 'Hall' Class 4-6-0 No 6934 *Beachamwell Hall*.

We alighted from the excursion at Reading West and made the 5-minute walk to the Western Region engine shed.

We then walked to Reading (Southern Region) engine shed. After this visit we walked the short distance to the General station where we purchased return tickets to Slough, for our third depot of the visit. We were steam-hauled to Slough by 'Hall' 4-6-0 No 5941 *Campion Hall*.

It is of note that *all* engines on shed at Slough were tank designs, the majority of these being used for hauling suburban trains to and from Paddington. The shed itself comprised five roads with a

BETWEEN READING AND SLOUGH

Steam locomotives:

1448	4090	4993	5037
5040	5080	5956	6029
6158	6844	6953	7914

BETWEEN SLOUGH AND READING

Steam locomotives:

4606	4921	4925	4979
4983	5035	5041	5066
5089	5763	5971	5979
6010	6108	6126	6134
6850	6929	6947	7017
7020	7022	7902	7906
31622	31869		

turntable adjacent to the coal stage.

We were steam-hauled between Slough and Reading General by 'Castle' Class 4-6-0 No 4079 *Pendennis Castle*.

We were then steam-hauled between Reading West and Basingstoke by Class '6100' 2-6-2 tank engine No 6153. At the station we noted Nos 30454, 34043 and 35025.

We then made the 5-minute walk to the depot, adjacent to the station and the main Waterloo to Southampton line. It had three roads, a very long yard

BASINGSTOKE DEPOT

Steam locomotives:

30160	30258	30368	30456
30457	30474	30488	30507
30515	30524	30724	30763
30790	31611	31633	34041
75075	75076	75079	

Diesel locomotives:
15232   15233

21 locomotives on shed

and several sidings.

A varied selection of classes were noted, most interesting being the class G6 0-6-0 tanks Nos 30160 and 30258, the latter being of 1894 vintage. All engines were in steam and in working order.

We were then steam-hauled between Basingstoke and Eastleigh by 'West Country' 4-6-2 No 34043 *Combe Martin*. The final stage to Fratton was by diesel units.

READING (SR) DEPOT

Steam locomotives:

30277	30521	30835	31616	31624	31625	31627	31630	31631	31635	31799	31806	33034
76053	76058	76059										

Diesel locomotives:
13271   13274

18 locomotives on shed

SLOUGH DEPOT

Steam locomotives:

1426	1474	3697	4638	4650	4691	5715	5766	6108	6115	6122	6136	6140
6146	6151	6152	6154	6157	6164	6664	9406	9421	9424	9781		

24 locomotives on shed

ISLE OF WIGHT

SUNDAY 13 APRIL

I was accompanied by railway enthusiast David Bodenham on this visit. Departure from Fratton station was at 2 pm, and we purchased return tickets to Ryde Pier Head. Our departure by ferry from Portsmouth Harbour was 2.35 pm. On our arrival at Ryde Pier Head we caught the petrol tram (standard gauge) to the Esplanade station; this tram line ran alongside the main railway tracks together with a wooden road, used for both pedestrians and cars, all being carried on a very long pier between the Pier Head and Esplanade stations. Walking up the steep roads leading to Ryde St Johns railway station, we made our way to Ryde locomotive depot, this walk taking us about 15 minutes.

This two-road straight shed was situated in very close proximity to the station and directly opposite the Works, which was responsible for repairs to the whole of the island's engines. Unfortunately, we could not obtain entrance to the workshops, but we did note the following three engines: 18, 24 and 35. No 18 was partially dismantled in the yard, No 24 was in ex-Works condition, whilst No 35 was in the Works and was noted through a gap in the main doors!

We then caught a train to Newport, the capital of the Isle of Wight, being steam-hauled by Class '02' 0-4-4 tank No 36 *Carisbrooke*.

Newport depot had officially closed at the end of 1957. It had two roads, one being a through road - the structure was very run down, with holes and gaps everywhere! The building was made of sheets of corrugated iron. There were no railway staff to be seen, but some clocking-in cards were noted still in situ.

All four of the Class '02' tanks were 'dead', but appeared to be in quite good external condition. All were inside the depot, probably awaiting duties for the coming week. The depot had numerous sidings, of which many had become overgrown with weeds.

We returned to Ryde, steam-hauled once again by *Carisbrooke*. Our return ferry departed at 7.35 pm.

This had been my first visit to both Ryde and Newport sheds and they were both 'all steam'. At the time of this visit, locomotives on the island totalled 21, and we noted all of them. All carried names of towns and villages in the island, and the accompanying list shows their class, number, name and introduction date.

---

70 H

RYDE DEPOT

Steam locomotives:

3	4	14	16
17	20	21	22
26	27	28	29
32	36		

14 locomotives on shed

Nos 3 and 4 were Class 'E1' 0-6-0 tanks, introduced 1874 to a Stroudley design. At this date these were the only remaining 'E1s' working in the island.

Remainder on shed were Class '02' 0-4-4 tanks, introduced 1923, with a water capacity in their tanks of 800 gallons.

70 G

NEWPORT DEPOT

Steam locomotives:

25	30	31	33

4 locomotives on shed

Class	No	Name	Introduced
E1	3	*Ryde*	1874
E1	4	*Wroxall*	1874
02	14	*Fishbourne*	1923
02	16	*Ventnor*	1923
02	17	*Seaview*	1923
02	18	*Ningwood*	1923
02	20	*Shanklin*	1923
02	21	*Sandown*	1923
02	22	*Brading*	1923
02	24	*Calbourne*	1923
02	25	*Godshill*	1923
02	26	*Whitwell*	1923
02	27	*Merstone*	1923
02	28	*Ashey*	1923
02	29	*Alverstone*	1923
02	30	*Shorwell*	1923
02	31	*Chale*	1923
02	32	*Bonchurch*	1923
02	33	*Bembridge*	1923
02	35	*Freshwater*	1923
02	36	*Carisbrooke*	1923

The Class 'E1' were of 0-6-0 wheel arrangement; all '02s' of 0-4-4 wheel arrangement.

WEYMOUTH, BOURNEMOUTH AND EASTLEIGH

SUNDAY 25 MAY

This was an excursion from Portsmouth Harbour station to Weymouth. Departure time was 10.15 am, and the return fare was £1. We were steam-hauled throughout by Fratton-allocated Class 'U' 2-6-0 No 31637.

At Weymouth we followed the footpath from the station to the engine shed, the walk taking us just over 10 minutes. The shed consisted of a three-road building with a single-track lifting shop and turntable.

SOUTHAMPTON, BOURNEMOUTH AND WEYMOUTH AREAS

Steam locomotives:

9620	30040	30087	30107
30108	30112	30548	30727
30764	30772	30781	30782
31632	34007	34009	34042
34044	34063	34093	34099
35021	35025	73114	76009
76016	76018	76027	

Returning to the station we used our return excursion ticket, catching a train to Bournemouth.

BETWEEN WEYMOUTH AND BOURNEMOUTH

Steam locomotives:
7011　　7033　　30860　　35029

Bournemouth Central had the longest platform on the Southern Region - 1,748 ft. We entered the depot yard via the end of the up platform; this was an excellent position for viewing the engine movements about the shed, which had four roads under cover, a lifting shop and a 65-foot turntable.

We then once again used our

BETWEEN BOURNEMOUTH AND EASTLEIGH

Steam locomotives:

30056	30229	30491	30778
35025	41318	73116	73117
75078			

return excursion tickets, catching a train from Bournemouth Central to Eastleigh. Our day ended by catching a steam-hauled train from Eastleigh to Fratton, travelling via Botley. The locomotive was Standard Class '4' 4-6-0 No 75079.

WEYMOUTH DEPOT

Steam locomotives:

1367	1368	1370	1418	1453	1459	1467	2815	3737	4133	4166	4624	5338
5384	5548	5784	5964	5978	5981	5997	6327	6344	6374	7780	7782	7924
8799	30532	30706	30707	30864	31614	31637	34019	34094				

35 locomotives on shed

Nos 1367/8/70 were Class '1366' 0-6-0 tank locomotives, introduced 1934. Collett development of Class '1361' saddle tank, but with panniers. These three were allocated to Weymouth especially for working the line to the harbour.

No 5548 was a Class '4500' 2-6-2 tank having minor repairs in the depot works.

BOURNEMOUTH DEPOT

Steam locomotives:

6991	30040	30057	30059	30060	30087	30093	30104	30106	30108	30111	30112	30127
30128	30260	30310	30324	30539	30541	30548	30690	30695	30727	30764	30772	30773
30782	30786	30865	31632	34007	34009	34018	34039	34040	34042	34043	34055	34093
34098	34099	34102	34105	34107	35020	35022	35026	73110	73117	75073	76016	76019

52 locomotives on shed   The Eastleigh list is at the top of the next page.

READING, OXFORD AND SWINDON

SUNDAY 8 JUNE

Our departure was from Fratton station on a Cardiff excursion at 10.30 am, and the return fare was 13/1d. I travelled with Eddie Rooke, David Bodenham, Terry Hunt, Charlie Best, Ian Gray, David Greenfield and Jack Knowler, all these being local railway enthusiasts. We were steam-hauled to Eastleigh by 'West Country' 4-6-2 No 34104 *Bere Alston*. On arrival at Eastleigh we

EASTLEIGH DEPOT

Steam locomotives:

77 S	30025	30029	30030	30032	30033	30037	30096	30105	30117	30125	30212	30285
30288	30289	30300	30316	30326	30328	30356	30376	30377	30378	30379	30473	30475
30476	30479	30480	30481	30504	30511	30515	30521	30523	30530	30535	30542	30543
30566	30765	30770	30771	30780	30783	30785	30787	30790	30791	30827	30838	30850
30851	30852	30853	30854	30855	30856	30857	30863	30864	30905	31620	31801	31803
32101	32491	32510	32556	32559	32579	33019	33020	33023	34008	34010	34058	34110
41293	41300	73112	75070	76007	76009	76010	76012	76017	76025	76026	76028	76057
76063	76067	76069	82012	82014	82015	82016						

Diesel locomotives:

13012	13014	D3469	15214	15230	15231	15232	15233	15234	15236

108 locomotives on shed

No 77 S was a Class 'C14' 0-4-0 tank locomotive, introduced 1923. Urie rebuild as a shunting engine of Drummond LSWR motor-train 2-2-0 which was originally introduced in 1906. Used as a Departmental engine at Redbridge Sleeper Works, Southampton, and allocated to Eastleigh.

---

alighted from the excursion and caught an ordinary service train to Basingstoke. We changed train once again at Basingstoke, and were then steam-hauled by Class '6100' 2-6-2 tank engine No 6162 to Reading West.

No 31325, noted between Fratton and Reading, was a Class 'P' 0-6-0 tank locomotive, intro-

BETWEEN FRATTON AND READING WEST

Steam locomotives:

4948	30454	30456	30457
30478	30724	30781	30789
31325	31806	33026	34063
35014			

duced 1909, and noted on shed at Winchester (sub-depot of Eastleigh). This small one-road shed was situated on the west side of the Southampton to Waterloo main line at Winchester City station. It only had room for one small tank engine.

Class '5600' 0-6-2 tank No 6643 was noted in ex-Works condition.

READING (WR) DEPOT

Steam locomotives:

1407	1447	2213	2815	2837	2882	3219	3738	3809	3810	3866	4606	4609
4661	4665	4960	4961	4969	4976	4995	4998	5061	5341	5763	5900	5901
5906	5924	5951	5956	5979	6101	6102	6103	6117	6126	6129	6130	6134
6150	6153	6161	6324	6327	6353	6387	6643	6853	6923	6953	7708	7821
7906	7914	7919	8430	9402	9424	9749	9791	90315				

Diesel locomotives:

13195	13196	13268	13269

Diesel railcars:

W29	W33	W38

68 locomotives on shed

It carried an 88C shedplate, being Barry, South Wales.

We next walked to Reading General station from where we caught a train to Oxford. We were steam-hauled by 'Grange' Class 4-6-0 No 6817 *Gwenddwr Grange*.

BETWEEN READING AND OXFORD

Steam locomotives:

2299	2815	3440	3653
3723	3866	4097	4147
4149	4941	5082	5083
5090	5386	6133	6822
7003	7927		

On arrival at Oxford we entered the depot via the end of the station platform - this was not the official entrance! Oxford was a timber-built depot consisting of four roads, a single-road repair shop and a long narrow yard running parallel with the main railway line. The former LMS depot was also noted (on the opposite side of the main line) - this long two-road structure was closed in the early 1950s, but was still standing at this date.

Eastern, Western, London Midland and sometimes Southern Region engines, together with Standards, were nearly always noted when passing this depot.

BETWEEN OXFORD AND SWINDON

Steam locomotives:

3780	4087	4088	5034
5312	5794	5997	6002
6373	6771	6839	6917
8432	8793	9772	61639

Diesel railcars:

W5	W6	W11	W15
W16	W32		

All above railcars except W32 were noted in a siding near Swindon Junction station, awaiting decision on withdrawal and possible use as 'spares' for other railcars.

81F OXFORD DEPOT

Steam locomotives:

1420	1435	1442	2236	2853	2880	2889	3805	3814	3822	3852	3857	4092
4902	4954	5012	5025	5033	5190	5378	5818	5952	5960	5966	5973	6111
6138	6152	6163	6304	6345	6821	7238	7239	7324	7411	7412	7760	7900
7911	7920	8106	8424	9475	9611	45376	48143	48196	48610	61058	75001	75029
80039	90355											

54 locomotives on shed

SWINDON WORKS

Steam locomotives:

1015	1019	1023	1140	1362	2249	2255	2834	2839	3040	3750	4080	4153
4174	4566	4612	4704	4916	4918	4921	4940	4951	4964	4984	4991	5004
5006	5010	5037	5040	5046	5057	5058	5067	5072	5088	5091	5094	5101
5411	5531	5710	5716	5926	5972	6000	6015	6025	6113	6343	6708	6727
6730	6762	6813	6825	6826	6861	6864	6877	6902	6904	6918	6922	6958
6969	7001	7004	7005	7006	7012	7024	7820	9304	9440	9610	9709	70020
70028	73036	78008	82020	82021	82033	82035	92194	92195	92196	92197		

Diesel locomotives:

D91	D92	D801	D802	13013	15100	15107	D3429	D2023	D2024	D2025	D2026

101 locomotives in works

No 1140 was a Class 'SHT' saddle-tank, introduced 1905 and used by the Swansea Harbour Trust; in for scrapping.

Class '9F' 2-10-0s Nos 92194-92197 were still being constructed.

After Oxford, we caught a train to Swindon.

We then returned home to Portsmouth travelling via Swindon Town, Marlborough and Andover Junction, being steam-hauled between Swindon Junction and Andover Junction by Standard Class '3' 2-6-2 tank No 82005 which was ex-Works from Swindon.

The two Class 'U' 2-6-0s, Nos

BETWEEN SWINDON AND ANDOVER JUNCTION

Steam locomotives:
4097	5039	5328	7017
8433	9772	31613	31629
34108			

Diesel railcar:
W4

31613 and 31629, were observed on passing the depot at Andover, a sub-depot of Eastleigh. Small and compact, its two roads could hold four engines under cover, with room for others in the sidings. It was unusual because it also adjoined a two-road GWR shed which in fact went out of use around the time of this visit; the shed shared the turntable located between their two buildings.

SHED CODES: A small oval plate displaying a number above a capital letter was carried by all BR steam locomotives, and was affixed to the smokebox door. The main depots were 'A', others then graded 'B', 'C', and so on. Sub-depots (where usually only a few engines could be seen) would not have a shed code, but would be a subsidiary of an 'A', 'B' or 'C' depot, etc.

For example, it was interesting to note an engine from Penzance (83G) on shed at Reading, and one often wondered what mileage some of these steam locomotives would achieve over a day or a weekend working. As already mentioned in one of the Swindon visits, ex-Works engines were used on 'running-in' duties, and it would be no surprise to note, for example, an engine from Wales being used on the Swindon to Andover line in the late 1950s, as we did on the trip mentioned above with No 82005. Another example of us being aware of shedplates was noting No 6643 (88C) - a Barry allocation at Reading depot.

PLYMOUTH, NEWTON ABBOT AND EXETER

SUNDAY 20 JULY

This was a Portsmouth Harbour station to Plymouth excursion, and the return fare was 30 shillings (including all fares). Departure was at 10.30 am.

We were steam-hauled as far as Salisbury by Class 'U' 2-6-0 No 31804.

A change of locomotive was made at Salisbury, the 'U' class being replaced by 'West Country' 4-6-2 No 34035 *Shaftesbury*.

Okehampton was a sub-depot of Exmouth Junction (72A) and con-sisted of a concrete block and

---

FRATTON, SOUTHAMPTON AND SALISBURY AREAS

Steam locomotives:
1014	30266	30274	30356
30448	30847	31613	31614
34029	34054	34104	35004
73112	76065	76068	

Diesel locomotive:
13012

---

asbestos single-line dead-end shed together with a 50-foot turntable.

On our arrival at Plymouth Friary station we walked up the platform and past the locomotive which had hauled us from Salisbury, No 34035 *Shaftesbury*. We proceeded to our first depot of visit, Plymouth (Friary), the former code being 72D.

We next walked to the main

SALISBURY, YEOVIL AND EXETER AREAS

Steam locomotives:
1021	1429	4145	5573
9439	30036	30044	30583
30667	30712	34031	34057
34060	34097	34109	35010
41295	41316	82017	82019

No 30583 was a Class '0415' 4-4-2 tank locomotive, introduced in 1882. Noted at Axminster station, employed on the Lyme Regis branch train.

PASSING OKEHAMPTON DEPOT

Steam locomotives:
31830	31831	31836	34032

Western Region depot, Laira; this walk via Heathfield Road and across some wasteland brought us

PASSING MELDON QUARRY

Steam locomotive:
30232

This class '02' 0-4-4 tank engine, introduced in 1889 and of Adams LSWR design, was allocated to Exmouth Junction. It was noted in the small one-road shed specially built to house the single small tank engine employed solely for working in the stone quarry sidings. This depot was situated 2 miles east of Okehampton, Devon, and was visible on passing, but only if you were aware of its location, as it could easily be passed by unnoticed! Meldon Quarry produces high-grade stone, which was ideally suitable for mainline ballast.

to the rear entrance. Friary had three lanes and was a through shed, whilst Laira had a large roundhouse and a four-lane shed.

We then made the 40-minute

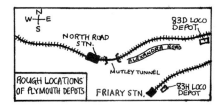

PLYMOUTH (FRIARY) DEPOT

Steam locomotives:
30034   30035   30036   30183
30192   31837   34002   34015
34057   34106   41315   41317

Diesel locomotives:
11225   11227   11228   11229

16 locomotives on shed

walk via Alexandra Road, Tavistock Road and St George's Street to Plymouth (North Road)

PLYMOUTH AND NEWTON ABBOT AREAS

Steam locomotives:
2261   3629   4092   4592
4992   5069   5096   5098
5967   5972   6016   6406
6837   6879   6938   7000
8451

Diesel locomotives:
D3509 D3510 D3516

station - according to the *Shed Directory*, this walk was 2 miles.

Newton Abbot was to be our next shed visit, and we were delighted to be steam-hauled by Collett-designed 'Manor' Class 4-6-0 No 7809 *Childrey Manor*.

On arrival at Newton Abbot we walked off the end of the platform and into the depot yard.

This depot, constructed of stone, consisted of six roads. The somewhat large works and repair shops at the rear of the depot proved to be of more interest to us than the depot. Two turntables were in close proximity, together with a traverser for works use.

The following ten engines were undergoing repairs in the workshop: 1449, 1468, 2206, 2209, 3705, 4179, 4569, 4619, D3513 and D3517.

Returning, via the end of the platform, to the station, we caught a diesel multiple unit train to Exeter (St David's).

BETWEEN NEWTON ABBOT AND EXETER

Steam locomotives:
4174   4905   5184   6943

LAIRA (PLYMOUTH) DEPOT

Steam locomotives:
1008	1361	1364	1421	1434	1650	2261	2811	2825	3639	3675	3686	3787
4086	4553	4590	4591	4656	4658	4679	4693	4701	4702	4976	4998	5085
5089	5106	5148	5175	5531	5567	5569	5572	5944	5956	6010	6016	6019
6024	6029	6407	6414	6419	6420	6421	6800	6801	6823	6842	6846	6849
6855	6859	6863	6871	6878	6940	6941	6956	6982	7029	7031	7333	7805
7812	7813	7820	7909	7916	8422	8425	8426	8709	9433	9467	9711	9716
9770	73020											

Diesel locomotives:
D600   D601   D3511   D3512   D3514   D3515   D3518   D3519   D3520   D3521   D3522   D3523

92 locomotives on shed

(83 A) NEWTON ABBOT DEPOT

Steam locomotives:

1003	1013	1022	1449	1452	1468	1472	1608	2206	2209	2809	2818	2827
2843	3600	3659	3705	3714	3773	3810	3834	3862	3864	4073	4083	4096
4098	4105	4117	4150	4176	4178	4179	4568	4569	4619	4932	4944	5007
5011	5024	5049	5079	5150	5154	5158	5164	5168	5178	5183	5195	5196
5336	5376	5533	5536	5573	5796	5904	5921	5942	6322	6384	6813	6829
6865	6938	6981	6989	6992	7010	7424	7808	7814	7815	8466	9440	9462
9487	9633	9668	9678	75002								

Diesel locomotives:
D3513 D3517

85 locomotives on shed

(83 C) EXETER DEPOT

Steam locomotives:

1429	1440	1451	1469	3603	3606	3677	3794	4081	4095	4985	4989	5339
5412	5959	5976	6365	6385	6869	7716	7809	8456	9439	9474	9497	9629
9765	48459											

28 locomotives on shed

PASSING EXMOUTH JUNCTION

Steam locomotives:
30129 32135

No 32135 was a Class 'E1/R' 0-6-2 tank engine, introduced in 1927 and employed on banking duty on the 1 in 37 incline between St David's and Central stations.

Exeter was a four-road shed with a single-road lifting shop and a turntable.

It was about 8 pm when we picked up the return excursion from Plymouth to Exeter Central.

This was my first visit to all these depots. The only main-line diesels noted during the entire day were Nos D600 *Active* and D601 *Ark Royal*. The party consisted of six.

NOTTINGHAM

SUNDAY 27 JULY

This was an excursion from Portsmouth Harbour station to Nottingham (Victoria). It was exactly one year ago that I had travelled to Nottingham on the corresponding excursion (Sunday 28 July 1957, page 39). The return fare was 18/9d (the 1957 fare had been 24/9d, which suggests that we purchased half-fares on this occasion!).

Departure was on time, at 10.12 am. We were steam-hauled to Eastleigh by Class 'T9' 4-4-0 locomotive No 30732 - it is of note that this was the same Fratton-allocated locomotive that hauled the excursion in 1957.

The 'T9' came off at Eastleigh and we were then steam-hauled by

FRATTON, EASTLEIGH and BASINGSTOKE

Steam locomotives:

DS681	DS3152	30199	30356
30376	30456	30536	30773
30779	30785	30806	30904
31325	31630	31804	31806
33031	34026	34045	34057
34068	34093	35015	35021
73110	73112		

Diesel locomotives:
15231 15236

'West Country' 4-6-2 locomotive No 34040 *Crewkerne*. On reaching Basingstoke this engine was replaced by 'Modified Hall' 4-6-0 locomotive No 7915 *Mere Hall*.

On passing Oxford shed (81F) we noted two Eastern Region Class 'B1' 4-6-0s, Nos 61055 and

READING, DIDCOT AND OXFORD AREAS

Steam locomotives:

1407	1442	2221	2222
3211	3814	3836	3848
4609	4954	5012	5094
5322	5332	5647	5930
6317	6327	6379	6864
6967	7312	7906	8430
9640	9653	30864	48544
61055	61369		

BANBURY AREA

Steam locomotives:

2270	2818	2856	3646
3861	5022	5407	5409
5420	80084	90069	92226

WOODFORD HALSE AND RUGBY AREAS

Steam locomotives:

43063	43067	44712	90312
90328	90474	90667	92164

LEICESTER AND NOTTINGHAM AREAS

Steam locomotives:

61455   63817   64827

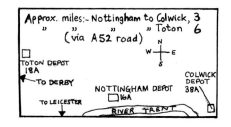

61369, London Midland Region Class '8F' 2-8-0 No 48544, a Southern Region 'Lord Nelson' and several unidentified Class 'WD' 2-8-0s in nearby sidings, once again proving that this depot and area could produce engines from all regions at one time.

Mere Hall was taken off at Banbury and we now had our fourth and final change of engine. We were quite surprised to note that we were then steam-hauled to our destination by Eastern Region Class 'B1' 4-6-0 No 61271.

Arrival at Nottingham (Victoria) was at 2.45 pm. We immediately donned our plastic macs and proceeded through the pouring rain to a nearby bus stop where we caught a bus to Toton, its destination being displayed as 'DERBY'. Toton was a large freight locomotive depot, situated on the west side of the main line between Long Eaton and Stapleford & Sandiacre railway stations. It was still raining as we entered the depot, which consisted of two buildings, containing three round-houses and a single-road through shed, presumably for servicing the former 'Beyer-Garratts' that were

too large for the turntables. The location also contained extensive sidings.

Toton's allocation of many heavy and powerful Class '8F' 2-8-0s and Standard Class '9F' 2-10-0s were specifically employed on long, heavily laden coal trains. Several years before this visit there were at Toton a batch of London Midland Region steam locomotives, unclassed but known as 'Beyer-Garratts' - their wheel arrangement was 2-6-6-2 (or simply 2-6-0 + 0-6-2) - and it was their job to haul the heavy coal trains from Toton sidings to Cricklewood in North London. They were first introduced in 1927 with fixed coal bunkers (two locomotives), and the remainder of the batch, about 30, were introduced in 1930 with rotary coal bunkers (capacity 9 tons) and other detail alterations. The 1927 versions weighed 148 tons 15 cwt and the 1930 versions

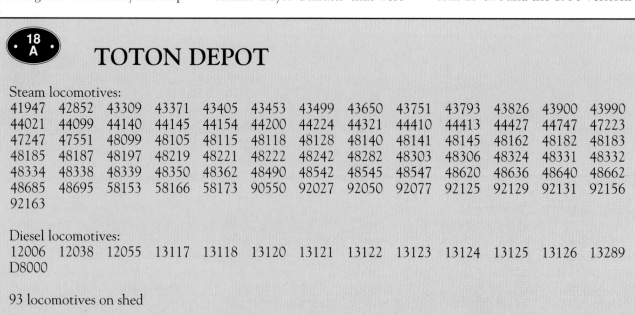

18A   # TOTON DEPOT

Steam locomotives:

41947	42852	43309	43371	43405	43453	43499	43650	43751	43793	43826	43900	43990
44021	44099	44140	44145	44154	44200	44224	44321	44410	44413	44427	44747	47223
47247	47551	48099	48105	48115	48118	48128	48140	48141	48145	48162	48182	48183
48185	48187	48197	48219	48221	48222	48242	48282	48303	48306	48324	48331	48332
48334	48338	48339	48350	48362	48490	48542	48545	48547	48620	48636	48640	48662
48685	48695	58153	58166	58173	90550	92027	92050	92077	92125	92129	92131	92156
92163												

Diesel locomotives:

12006	12038	12055	13117	13118	13120	13121	13122	13123	13124	13125	13126	13289
D8000												

93 locomotives on shed

155 tons 10 cwt.

To provide a huge boiler and a deep firebox within the limits of the British loading gauge, these locomotives were double ended; they had two sets of cylinders and driving wheels and carried the very large boiler slung between them. Two water tanks were provided, 2,700 gallons on the forward and 1,800 on the rear locomotive bogie. Thus the 'Beyer-Garratts' were two 2-6-0s in one, and this cut down the need to have coal trains double-headed; thus only one crew was required instead of two. This type of locomotive has also been widely used in overseas countries of the British Commonwealth. The complete batch of 'Beyer-Garratts' was withdrawn from British Railways by the mid-1950s. None of the batch was saved for preservation.

Also visited, by bus, were the depots at COLWICK (38A) and NOTTINGHAM (16A), both of which I had visited during July 1957. Colwick had 142 steam locomotives on shed, whilst Nottingham had 86, of which 12 were 0-6-0 diesel shunters.

Colwick, with its predominately freight engine allocation that at one time included about 60 'WD' 2-8-0s, was visited without a permit. The rear wall of the depot formed part of Victoria Road, and we made our entrance by climbing over a low-roofed cycle shed to avoid going 'through the offices'. The shed was very smoky due to the direction of the wind, visibility inside being extremely restricted. We completed our visit without being stopped.

DONCASTER

SATURDAY 30 AUGUST TO MONDAY 1 SEPTEMBER

This was a rail/coach trip from Portsmouth to Doncaster via London, and engine sheds and works were visited on both the forward and the return journey. I went on this trip with local railway enthusiasts Jim 'Jimpy' Lawrence, Charlie Best, Jack Knowler and David Greenfield. This coach trip was organised by Mr Ernie Middleton of the London (King's Cross) Locospotters Club, whose address was obtained through reading the 'clubs and visits' columns of a monthly railway journal. The coach was scheduled to depart from York Way, adjacent to King's Cross station, at 8.15 am on Sunday 31 August.

The first train from Portsmouth to London on that Sunday would not get us to our departure point in time, so it was decided to leave Portsmouth on Saturday and sleep the night on King's Cross station. The cost of travel on the coach between London and Doncaster was not recorded, but the overall spending cash, which included food and drinks and the single train fare from Fratton to London

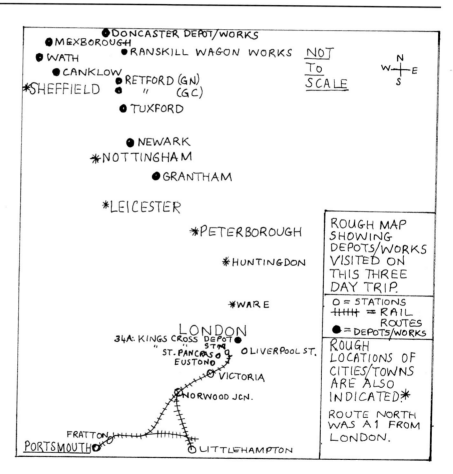

(Victoria), amounted to £3.

SATURDAY 30 AUGUST (Day 1)

I departed from Fratton station at 12.30 pm with Jim Lawrence and Charlie Best. Jack Knowler and

David Greenfield did not travel with us, but travelled on a later train and stayed with relatives in London overnight. We had arranged to meet them at King's Cross station during Saturday evening. We purchased single tickets to London (Victoria).

12, Eade Road,
Harringay,
London N.4.
24th June 1958

Dear M,

    Thank you for your letter and enquiries.

    I have had many many chaps from Portsmouth on our trips, and some still come. Anyhow I welcome your friends and hope to see many of them.

    It is a pity you have that long wait for the coach on August 31st. There are many Youth hostels in London, could you not sleep there ?

    The coach leaves Kings Cross (York Way) about 8.15 and there are in York Way several cafes which open early so that you can get tea if you wish.

    I am enclosing two fixture lists and if you require any more you can let me know. If you and your friends are definite, please forward the required deposits to Mr. Hall address stated in the list.

    On August Bank Holiday, we are visiting S.W.Scotland and I am allowing several youngsters to go for £5 odd. If any of your friends desire to take advantage, kindly let me know at your earliest convenience. All hotels and some meals paid for.

Yours truly,

E.R.Middleton,

A letter I received from Mr Ernie Middleton answering queries about Doncaster trip.

FRATTON, CHICHESTER, HORSHAM AND LONDON AREAS

Steam locomotives:
4962	30054	30055	30839
31145	31578	31639	31807
31860	32448	32469	32498
32650	34048	34092	76053
80032			

Diesel locomotive:
13271

These 0-6-2 tanks of Class 'N2' were to be seen whenever a visit to King's Cross station or depot was made.

We then visited King's Cross station.

Our next station was Liverpool Street, and we travelled there by tube train. At some point on our journey we surfaced on to BR lines and noted steam locomotive No 69593, diesel shunter No 12129 and electric locomotive (London Transport) No 7 *Edmund Burke*.

We later met up with Jack and David who were to accompany us on the coach trip to Doncaster. After a brief meeting, in which we told them that we had visited stations, they

EUSTON

Steam locomotives:
40042	40054	40060	42366
44497	44873	45242	45525
45532	45629	45647	46154
46256	47302	47495	47668
47671	48324	70044	

Diesel locomotives:
10001 D8002

ST PANCRAS

Steam locomotives:
40039　44777　45253　45569

KING'S CROSS

Steam locomotives:
60003	60012	60048	60059
60102	60110	60111	60122
60123	60158	60506	60520
60800	60829	60971	60974
61090	61113	61282	67744
67770	67772	67783	67794
67797	69491	69493	69498
69516	69522	69524	69528
69532	69539	69543	69547
69575	69586	69592	

LIVERPOOL STREET

Steam locomotives:
61096	61119	61227	61336
61615	61631	61640	61672
61849	61989	62066	62070
67720	67732	67734	68619
69603	69614	69622	69627
69633	69634	69646	69663
69666	69668	69670	69712
69715	69721	69723	70000
70003	70005	70008	70010
70011	70039		

Diesel locomotives:
D200	D202	D204	D205
D5512			

It was agreed that we visit Euston, St Pancras, King's Cross and Liverpool Street stations prior to meeting up with Jack and David at King's Cross station later that evening.

We then made the 5-minute walk along Euston Road to St Pancras. The engines listed were noted during several visits in the afternoon and evening.

both left us and made their way to their relatives' house for the night. We made sure that they knew that the meeting time in York Way on

Sunday morning was to be 8 am. Our base for the night was to be King's Cross station, on the longest platform, and our beds consisted of porters' trolleys with our haversacks as pillows. At about 11 pm we decided to try and get some sleep, but with trains coming in and out of the station it was almost impossible.

Charlie Best had only a plastic mac covering him as he lay on the trolley, but he fell asleep almost instantly, sleeping for nearly three hours! Jim Lawrence and myself could only manage about 30 minutes' sleep - whilst Charlie was snoring we walked to and from St Pancras stations several times, consuming cartons of milk and bars of chocolate from the station vending machines. We returned to the platform several times to find Charlie fast asleep amidst much hissing of steam and movements of engines. After three hours he suddenly awoke, sat up and casually said 'Where am I?'.

It was just after 2 am that Jim and I eventually fell asleep but we were woken just before 4 am by the sound of an engine's whistle. The first signs of daylight were beginning to appear, yet it seemed as though we had only just got our heads down! The amount of activity at the station during the night really surprised us - trains were flitting in and out at regular intervals. Weatherwise, it had been quite warm - in fact, we all slept with just our plastic macs covering us. We did find that having haversacks as pillows was rather uncomfortable: being loaded with food and drink, books, pens and a transistor radio, mine proved to be rather lumpy! One of the books which I always carried with me was the Ian Allan Combined Volume *ABC of British Railways Locomotives* Winter 1956/7 edition, which at this date cost 10/6d.

The engines listed on the right were noted during the night at King's Cross station.

Only three steam locomotives were noted at EUSTON during the night visits: 45578, 47307 and 47315.

SUNDAY 31 AUGUST (Day 2)

No railway officials had approached us regarding our 'kip' on the platform. Breakfast comprised of several cheese sandwiches and a drink of orange squash! We walked out of the station and along York Way to King's Cross depot; the time as we entered the shed was 5.40 am - we did not have a permit.

The depot consisted of separate eight-road and seven-road sheds and a repair works, with numerous sidings adjacent.

At this date 34A had 125 steam and 23 diesel shunters in its allocation, 19 of the former being Class 'A4' streamlined 'Pacifics' used on

---

KING'S CROSS

Steam locomotives:

60026	60030	60055	60064
60070	60107	60110	60115
60117	60134	60142	60523
60820	60871	60902	61027
61075	61091	61097	61200
61393	61912	67745	67749
67794	68906	68928	68982
69491	69522	69531	69546
69552	69556	69561	69577
69586	69589	69592	69644
73158	92196		

Diesel locomotive:
D3444

34A   KING'S CROSS DEPOT

Steam locomotives:

60003	60007	60012	60015	60016	60021	60022	60028	60030	60034	60039	60044	60059
60062	60065	60072	60105	60107	60108	60109	60117	60122	60134	60139	60142	60156
60157	60506	60532	60533	60800	60832	60846	60847	60850	60862	60930	60941	60976
61075	61139	61200	61247	61300	61364	64175	67767	67768	67770	67774	67779	67783
67792	67797	68921	68987	69498	69499	69504	69506	69512	69517	69520	69521	69523
69526	69528	69535	69536	69540	69544	69545	69548	69549	69569	69570	69575	69579
69580	69581	69583	69584	69585	69589	69593	73157	73159	92039	92040	92142	92143
92172	92173	92174	92181									

Diesel locomotives:

12112	D3165	13307	13309	13310	13334	D3440	D3441	D3442	D3450	D3474	D3475	D3476

108 locomotives on shed

the main-line expresses to Scotland.

On returning to King's Cross station we had hot drinks and sandwiches and then met up with Jack Knowler and David Greenfield. We were both quite sleepy after a somewhat restless night, but we did manage to board the coach at 8 am - I recollect passing through Ware, Hertfordshire, and seeing a diesel shunter in some sidings, but then sleep overcame me.

This trip to Doncaster was a 'one off' affair. Some of the locomotives that were noted at the depots visited would most likely never be seen again, this being partly because of their age and partly because another visit to these Eastern Region depots would never be made again. A camera would have been the answer to capture some of these classes, but none of us gave it a thought at the time. Therefore in this particular 'one off' trip, to illustrate some of the interesting and some of the ancient locomotives noted, I have added some simple drawings; they are not necessarily to scale or show all external details, but represent a rough indication of the locomotives' appearance.

When I awoke I found that the coach had arrived at Grantham engine shed entrance. Grantham depot was a four-road straight shed with a block end.

I don't think our organiser, Mr

The first of my drawings is of a Class 'C12' 4-4-2 'Atlantic' tank engine, introduced in 1898 and still in working order when seen at Grantham. It was an Ivatt GN design, and was easily identified by its smokebox being set well back from its front buffer beam.

Ernie Middleton, had permits for all of the depots to be visited. He certainly did not at Grantham, as the shed foreman was seen running up the yard shouting out 'Who's in charge?'. There were 35 in our coach party and Ernie was leading; nobody had stopped to inform the shed foreman that we had arrived - the party just carried on walking. On leaving we passed his office and saw him muttering to himself - he was obviously not very happy!

The coach then continued to our next depot, Tuxford, a small three-road through depot. Its allocation of approximately 15 locomotives would probably fill the building.

The coach then continued, but stopped at a transport cafe where we purchased baked beans on toast and cups of tea and chocolate biscuits. We then headed towards Doncaster, to Retford (Great Central) depot, which was situated

TUXFORD DEPOT

Steam locomotives:
```
63597   63635   63643   63665
63667   63691   63722   63893
63912   64333   64346   64354
64364   64450
```

14 locomotives on shed

on the south side of the Retford to Gainsborough railway line and consisted of three roads, two being through roads and one a block end.

On leaving the depot the coach then took us to the nearby Retford (Great Northern) depot, only about 700 yards away. This depot

A Class '1P' 0-4-4 tank engine, introduced in 1889. This was a Johnson Midland design, and was 'push-and-pull' fitted, ideal for light passenger work. No 58065 was on shed at Retford GN and I 'cabbed' it.

GRANTHAM DEPOT

Steam locomotives:
```
60047   60049   60061   60082   60106   60149   60153   60513   60524   60821   60856   60893   60909
60914   60963   61389   61419   61467   61771   61966   63923   63929   63930   63931   63938   63940
63948   63960   63966   64181   64246   67352   67800   68626   68638   68866   69550   69814   69827
90458   92183   92187   92188
```

43 locomotives on shed

RETFORD (GC) DEPOT

Steam locomotives:
63637   63688   63782   63785
63905   63914   63925   63944
63961   63970   63971   63972
64188   64241   64259   64283
64348   64395   64416   64421
64423   64451   64759   68502
90400   90647

26 locomotives on shed

RETFORD (GN) DEPOT

Steam locomotives:
58065   61126   61193   61212
61213   63736   63818   63965
63986   64287   64830   64893
64906   64908   64961   64970
68498   68508   68530   69314
69322

Diesel locomotives:
D3614 D3618

23 locomotives on shed

carried the same code as the Central depot and was situated west of Retford railway station; it consisted of four roads and was a block-end type.

While at RETFORD STATION we noted Nos 60070, 60113 and 60872.

The coach then continued to our next installation, this being RANSKILL WAGON WORKS, situated on the southern outskirts

Another ancient tank class, the 'N5' 0-6-2 of 1891, of which two, Nos 69314 and 69322, were on the GN shed.

of Doncaster. There we saw two steam locomotives, Nos 3 and 4; these unusual small four-wheeled types had been transferred to Departmental use, this location being an ideal area for their employment on light shunting and the slow moving of wagons in the extensive yards. Their weight, just over 20 tons, also made them useful for light dock shunting and other miscellaneous duties.

The coach then continued to our destination, Doncaster, dropping us off at the station.

Doncaster was a 12-road through straight shed with turning facilities by means of a triangle to the north-east side. It had an allocation of nearly 200 locomotives at one time and was destined to become the last steam shed on the Eastern Region.

The party of 35 then visited Doncaster Works. The following details about the Works were made known to us during our visit: the area covered was 84 acres, and more than 2,200 steam locomotives had been built here, the final

DONCASTER DEPOT

Steam locomotives:
48360   60004   60046   60056   60073   60082   60104   60112   60125   60518   60700   60841   60843
60852   60874   60889   60917   60921   60936   60943   60956   60960   61036   61114   61122   61124
61128   61145   61157   61162   61196   61225   61326   61800   61807   61812   61829   61887   61892
61895   61905   61929   61961   61964   61972   62024   62048   62061   62599   63618   63744   63855
63869   63906   63924   63926   63939   63943   63945   63955   63956   63962   63964   63967   63968
63969   63978   63979   63981   63983   63984   63985   63987   64179   64185   64232   64258   64262
64270   64721   64737   64810   64838   64876   64883   64898   64947   64966   64981   67785   67794
68022   68069   68071   68507   68520   68556   68558   68569   68587   68621   68654   68869   68892
68896   68926   68960   68980   90075   90255   90537   90550   90602   90636   92169   92170   92175
92177   92189   92196

Diesel locomotives:
D3140 D3480 D3482 D3484 D3619

125 locomotives on shed

Nos 68022/69/71 were Class 'J94' 0-6-0 saddle tanks bought from the Ministry of Supply in 1946.

DONCASTER WORKS

Steam locomotives:
43070 60023 60025 60029 60033 60036 60037 60042 60054 60057 60058 60063 60066
60067 60081 60100 60116 60123 60128 60143 60148 60154 60511 60528 60530 61094
61121 61125 61137 61185 61208 61289 61328 61600 61605 61606 61630 61634 61643
61843 61845 61862 61954 62010 62038 63951 63952 64219 64220 64227 64244 64255
64261 64263 64267 64275 68800 68842 68847 68848 68924 69472 69527 69530 69554
73046 73048

Diesel locomotives:
 D208 11108 11219 D2004 D2045 D2046 D2047 13138 D3139 13154 D3318 D3377 D3655
D3684 D3685 D3686 D5511

Electric locomotives:
E5000 E5001 E5002

87 locomotives in Works

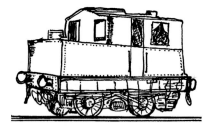

Class 'Y3' 0-4-0.

Unique Class 'W1' 'Baltic' 4-6-4 No 60700, which was on shed at Doncaster; this was the first time I had noted this locomotive. Originally numbered 10000 and introduced on trials in 1929, Gresley involved the firm of Yarrow in this design, which resulted in an experimental four-cylinder compound with a water-tube boiler at a pressure of 450 lb per sq in. It was the most powerful locomotive in Britain, but was rebuilt in 1937 into a conventional three-cylinder engine. Its streamlined casing made it look very similar to Gresley's 'A4' 4-6-2s. Total weight: 168 tons 14 cwt. Driving wheels: 6 ft 8 in.

one in 1957. Some of the most famous named steam locomotives were built here, such as Nos 60014 *Silver Link*, 60022 *Mallard* and 60103 *Flying Scotsman*.

Named main-line passenger and mixed traffic types were much in evidence, and the three electric locomotives were under construction for the Southern Region. We had a permit for our visit.

Emerging from the main workshops we then entered DONCASTER WORKS YARD

where we saw Class 'J52/2' 0-6-0 saddle tanks Nos 1 and 2. Introduced in 1897 they were former British Railways Nos 68845 and 68816 respectively. We also saw No 5, a Class 'Y3' 0-4-0 Sentinel Wagon Works design. It was two-speed geared, and had been introduced in 1927. Its former British Railways number was 68185. No 4 (68181) of this class had been noted at Ranskill.

Leaving the Doncaster area, the coach travelled south-west to our

next depot, Mexborough.

It is noteworthy that there were no fewer than 24 Class 'WD' 2-8-0s at this shed. It was a very large shed, consisting of 15 roads; it had a block end. At this date it had about 90 locomotives in its allocation, over 40 of which were Class 'WD' 2-8-0s - another shed with a predominantly freight engine allocation.

The coach then continued to Wath depot, this being a sub-depot of Mexborough. If I remember rightly, Wath was quite a large straight shed, comprising about six roads.

All the electric locomotives seen there were Class 'EM1' Bo-Bos introduced in 1950 to a Metropolitan-Vickers and Gresley design for the LNER; the current

MEXBOROUGH DEPOT

Steam locomotives:
48089 61112 61165 61167 61850 63586 63604 63625 63668 63672 63673 63701 63723
63728 63753 63756 63757 63791 63798 63807 63812 63813 63835 63841 63843 63845
63850 63851 63876 63891 63894 63897 63898 64393 64402 64406 64987 69308 90139
90153 90190 90209 90211 90220 90223 90250 90270 90311 90330 90410 90421 90441
90506 90521 90526 90567 90587 90597 90612 90668 90670 90700

Diesel locomotive:
13335

63 locomotives on shed

WATH DEPOT

Diesel locomotives:
13062 D3063 13064

Electric locomotives:
26003 26004 26006 26009
26011 26012 26017 26028
26030 26032 26038 26039
26040 26044 26045 26046
26047 26050 26055

22 locomotives on shed

Class 'EM1' Bo-Bo electric locomotive.

collection was from overhead catenary. The original member of this class, No 26000 (not noted), was introduced in 1941 and named *Tommy*; 57 others followed. The depot of allocation of all 58 locomotives was Reddish.

The three diesels noted were all 0-6-0 shunters. This was the first 'non-steam' depot that I had ever visited.

We were now on the return journey south, towards London. The coach stopped and we visited Canklow, a depot which came under the Sheffield area codes of the London Midland Region. This depot, like so many of the previous ones visited on this trip, proved to have a majority of freight types in its allocation. Situated in Rotherham, Canklow depot consisted of a single-building roundhouse.

The final depot visited on this

A Class '3F' 0-6-0 locomotive, introduced in 1885. Nine of this class, numbered between 43180 to 43814, were on shed at Canklow.

A Class '1F' 0-6-0 tank locomotive, introduced in 1878. Two of this class, Nos 41835 and 41875, were seen at Canklow. Note the cut-back cab.

CANKLOW DEPOT

Steam locomotives:
41835 41875 43180 43225 43361 43369 43371 43660 43664 43753 43814 44082 44128
44206 44334 47238 47546 47547 48026 48115 48138 48140 48319 48377 48391 48397
48407 48638 48704 58146 58170 58198 78026 90384 90582

35 locomotives on shed

coach trip was Newark, a sub-depot of Retford. This was a very small straight shed, with only two or three roads. Here I 'cabbed' Class '1P' 0-4-0 tank engine No 58085.

NEWARK DEPOT

Steam locomotives:
58085 64174 64178 64234
64236 90108

6 locomotives on shed

Whilst on the way back to London the coach was held up in a traffic jam for more than two hours! We eventually arrived back in York Way, King's Cross, very late in the evening at around 11.20 pm - too late to get across to either Victoria or Waterloo to catch the last train home back to Portsmouth. We said goodbye to Jack and David who, on arrival at York Way, decided to stay the night at their relatives' house once again. Myself, Charlie Best and Jim Lawrence decided that another night on King's Cross station platform would be the best way to spend the night.

We purchased hot drinks and chocolates from a vending machine and then adjourned to the porters' trolleys at the far end of the longest platform. It did not take us very long to settle down, once again using our haversacks as pillows. Train activity did not seem as busy as it had on Saturday, perhaps because it was now Sunday - we had all fallen asleep just before midnight.

MONDAY 1 SEPTEMBER (Day 3)

The following steam locomotives were noted during the very early hours at King's Cross: Nos 60044, 60136, 60142, 60908, 60976,

67773, 68906, 69498, 69530, 69533, 69548 and 69577.

The station clock showed 5.50 am as we awoke. We gathered up our haversacks and immediately prepared to make our way home to Portsmouth - we had purchased single tickets on the forward journey on Saturday, and this procedure would now be repeated for the homeward trip. However, on counting up our money it was found that certain of us did not have enough cash to get home, or anywhere near Portsmouth - we had spent quite a few shillings purchasing numerous drinks and chocolates from the station vending machines.

A short discussion was held at King's Cross station, the outcome of which was that some of the party, who shall remain anonymous, decided to make their way to Fratton via the 'Charlie Best route'. This was a method devised by Charlie, whereby any railway enthusiast could travel from London to Portsmouth or vice versa free of charge, or sometimes at just the cost of a platform ticket! The method entailed travelling on specific trains, which only we local railway enthusiasts would recognise, and also changing trains at various selected stations on a route that was anything but direct!

Apparently, on departure from King's Cross by tube train the party eventually emerged at ground level to find themselves at New Cross Gate, a British Railways SR station. Alighting there, but remaining on the same platform, they caught a non-corridor electric suburban unit train to Norwood, where they again alighted. Remaining on the platform, they next picked up another non-corridor electric unit train bound for Horsham, where they changed train once again.

They were now travelling on a Victoria to Littlehampton train.

As this was a corridor train they separated, travelling in the toilets to avoid being seen by any ticket inspector who may have been on the train. On arrival at Littlehampton, a terminus, they remained on the train until it departed; when they eventually arrived at Barnham they alighted and once again remained on the same platform.

They now boarded their final train home to Fratton. They were very careful to board a Brighton-Portsmouth stopping train - to be precise the fourth carriage of a non-corridor electric unit train. On arrival at Fratton they alighted to find that, as anticipated, their carriage had stopped exactly opposite the entrance to the gentlemen's toilet, to which they immediately went. They remained there until the ticket collector at the barrier returned to his room on the platform, then their final exit was made, individually, up the steps, over the footbridge and out of the station. A train standing at platform 1 shielded them as they made their way up the stairs.

They arrived home at about 10 am, some hours after the rest of us, very tired but much relieved that the 'Charlie Best route' had proved to be a success for them,

BETWEEN NEW CROSS GATE AND FRATTON VIA LITTLEHAMPTON

Steam locomotives:
30056 30109 30546 30693
31162 31575 31763 31863
31921 32411 32445 32451
32484 32528 32532 32544
32548 32552 32557 32564
32650 33002 33035 42070
76062

Diesel locomotives:
D3013 13221 D3222 13223
13271 15214

bearing in mind their financial embarrassment.

Only nine main-line diesels were noted during the entire trip. It is of note that some diesels at this date were being renumbered with the prefix 'D' denoting diesel, this taking the place of the figure '1', the change being carried out as they went to works for overhaul.

Steam locomotives dating from the 1880s and 1890s were common at most of the depots visited and the majority of these were in working order. Main-line locomotives included Classes 'A1', 'A2', 'A3' and 'A4' together with

numerous Class 'B1' 4-6-0s and 'V2' 2-6-2s. It is of note that of the 184 members of the latter class, only seven carried a name; of these we noted three, Nos 60800 *Green Arrow*, 60847 *St Peter's School, York, AD 627* and 60872 *King's Own Yorkshire Light Infantry*. If you think that these nameplates must have been rather lengthy, another of the class, No 60835 (not noted on this trip), carried the name *The Green Howard, Alexandra, Princess of Wales's Own Yorkshire Regiment* - surely the longest nameplate ever carried by a British Railways steam locomotive!

To sum up, it had been an extremely memorable trip, not only for the steam engines noted, the locations visited and the 'sleeping rough' on King's Cross station, but also for the details I subsequently learned of the free 'Charlie Best route'!

On my arrival home I went straight to bed, taking only my shoes off! I recollect my mother bringing me up some beans on toast and a cup of tea; I drank the tea then sleep overcame me. I awoke several hours later to find baked beans scattered all over my bed!

ADDITIONAL HIGHLIGHTS OF 1958

A MID-WINTER MIDLANDS ESCAPADE!

As the reader will already have gathered from this book, Portsmouth contained a great number of train-spotters of varied ages and groupings, and engine shed visits up and down the country were taking place on a regular basis. Although this book sets out to deal primarily with my own experiences, I feel it is appropriate to detail below a somewhat 'out of the ordinary' trip undertaken by Eddie Rooke which I have always regretted missing out on.

Eddie attended Portsmouth Southern Grammar School for Boys which possessed a very active railway club. Having started up as a model railway club, it was soon transformed by Eddie and David Copus into a very thriving train-spotting club. In fact, so popular did it become that within a very short time it had the highest membership of pupils of any club within the school! Fortunately I was able to participate in several of

their trips, although I of course attended a different school. Prior to the Christmas holidays, plans had been drawn up by some members of the club, including Eddie, Charlie Best, 'Gaffer' Bleach and Terry Hunt (who attended Southsea Modern School), to visit the Midlands over the first three days of 1958. Although the finer details of the trip are restricted to Eddie's list of locomotives seen, it is well worth recalling that this three-day trip was undertaken by a group of ten youths aged between 13 and 16 years of age, most of whom had never been away from home overnight before, with no sleeping arrangements having been made for the two nights away.

WEDNESDAY 1 JANUARY: At that date, not being a public holiday, trains were running a normal weekday service, and with the Works open that afternoon SWINDON was first visited, travelling via Reading. New engines under construction in the Works at that time were Class '9F' 2-10-0s Nos 92184, 92185 and 92186, and diesel shunters Nos 11194 to 11201.

WORCESTER DEPOT (85A) was then visited after travelling via Didcot and Oxford, but being without a permit the party was ejected before completing the visit. They then moved on to KIDDERMINSTER DEPOT (85D) before ending up at Wolverhampton (Low Level) station, where they planned to spend the night in the platform waiting room.

It would seem that everyone had succeeded in getting to sleep, but at about midnight they were all awakened by a visit from the police, and it was pointed out that they could not stay on the station platform overnight. The police insisted that the party accompany an officer to the local police station where an attempt would be made to find them overnight accommodation.

Surprisingly enough, transport in the form of a 'Black Maria' was provided, but on arrival at the police station it soon became evident that it would not be possible to find accommodation at that time of night. Accordingly, much to their credit, the police provided cells with bunk beds overnight, fed their guests with doughnuts and hot chocolate drinks, and provided an early alarm call for 6 am so that they could start their engine shed visits early!

THURSDAY 2 JANUARY: The second day commenced with a visit to WOLVERHAMPTON (STAFFORD ROAD) DEPOT (84A) and WORKS. This was followed by OXLEY DEPOT (84B) - where a surprising visitor was 'Pug' 0-4-0 saddle tank No 51204 - then ex-LMS depots BUSHBURY (3B), WALSALL (3C) and BESCOT (3A).

STOURBRIDGE JUNCTION DEPOT (84F) was next to be visited and although Eddie still has photographs taken at this location they are regrettably not of good quality, since at that time he was interested in photography and was developing and printing his own films, with very mixed results!

With night beginning to fall, TYSELEY DEPOT (84E) was visited, followed by the last visit of the day, MONUMENT LANE (3E), where 'Compound' 4-4-0s No 40936 and 41090 were in store. At this time snow was beginning to fall, and having been warned by the Wolverhampton police that they would take a very dim view if they were called out to attend to them again, the party decided upon a new strategy based upon the theory that the police only visited railway stations just after pub closing times to move on drunks and tramps - and if they were to arrive at the station some time after midnight they should get an interruption-free night.

Accordingly they all went to the pictures that night to see *The Pride and the Passion* starring Sophia Loren and Cary Grant; afterwards they wandered the streets for an hour or so, in freezing temperatures, before spending the night on Birmingham (New Street) station - without any problems.

FRIDAY 3 JANUARY: Day three started with a visit just before 6 am to SALTLEY DEPOT (21A) which was jammed tight with predominantly freight locomotives. This was followed by ASTON DEPOT (3D) before the party started heading southwards and home, visiting on the way LEAMINGTON SPA DEPOT (84D), where a few people were puzzled by the presence of stationary boiler No 2067, a Class '2021' 0-6-0 pannier tank withdrawn many years earlier. The final visits on the way home were BANBURY DEPOT (84C), OXFORD DEPOT (81F), DIDCOT DEPOT (81E) and READING DEPOT (81D).

All in all it was quite a memorable adventure - considerably different from anything any of my friends had tackled before.

LONDON: 9 FEBRUARY - London depots were visited for the first time on a Sunday. Due to engineering work on the line at Hilsea, between Fratton and Havant, the train we had planned to use, the 6.20 am to Waterloo, was cancelled. We therefore caught a double-decker bus from Fratton station forecourt to Havant, the guard blowing his whistle to start the bus off! This was found to be the usual practice on future such trips whenever a bus was used.

Noted on shed at BRICKLAYERS ARMS (73B) was the 'Battle of Britain' locomotive No 34066 *Spitfire*; this Bulleid-designed 4-6-2

was the one that had been involved in the Lewisham rail disaster on 4 December 1957, which happened in dense fog. The steam train involved was the late-running 4.56 pm Cannon Street to Ramsgate express which collided with the rear of the ten-carriage electric unit train forming the 5.18 pm Charing Cross to Hayes. The impact, with the steam train travelling at 30 mph, brought down part of the Nunhead Viaduct, resulting in 90 passenger fatalities; the guard of the electric train was also killed. *Spitfire* was extensively damaged, and was moved to the nearby Bricklayers Arms depot to await a decision on its future. Judging by its external appearance on this visit we thought that it would be irreparable.

LONDON: 27 APRIL - Another Sunday visit. No fewer than 15 Class 'C' 0-6-0s were seen at HITHER GREEN, one of the main depots in the South East where these aging engines could be seen in steam and in active use. No 31461 was on shed having suffered damage when it was involved in a collision with an electric train

A Class 'C' 0-6-0, a Wainwright design for the SE&CR.

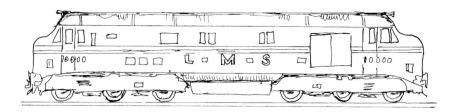

Diesel-electric locomotive No 10000, seen at Willesden.

at Greenwich several weeks prior to this visit. This class was introduced in 1900.

Moving on to WILLESDEN (1A) we noted diesel-electric main-line locomotives Nos 10000 and 10001, introduced in 1947 and 1948 respectively. No 10000 had the distinction of being the first main-line diesel locomotive on British Railways.

A visit to PLAISTOW shed (33A) saw 41 steam locomotives on shed, of which 13 were comparatively new Standard tanks, having only been built in the early 1950s.

BRISTOL AND BATH: 17 AUGUST - Another Sunday excursion. I travelled with Eddie Rooke, David Copus, Frank Allen and Timothy Julnes. We were steam-hauled between Salisbury and Bristol by 'Castle' No 4075

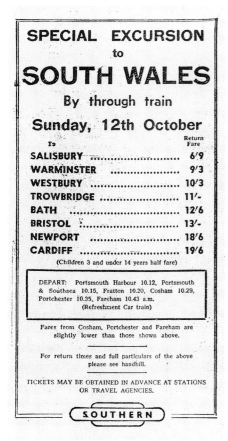

An advertisement, identical to that for the trip described here, but for Sunday 12 October 1958.

Cardiff Castle. Class '4500' 2-6-2 tank engine No 5532 was noted in the single-road Bath shed, this being a sub-shed of Bristol (Bath Road) (82A) - the oddity of this building was that it had a water tank for its roof. Depots visited were: BARROW ROAD (82E) with 46 steam and two diesels; BATH ROAD (82A) with 66 steam; ST PHILIPS MARSH (82B) with 76 steam, 18 diesel shunters and three railcars and; for the first time BATH (GREEN PARK) shed.

BATH (GREEN PARK) DEPOT

Steam locomotives:

34097	40601	40696	40698
40700	41242	41243	42754
44096	44463	44558	44559
44560	44561	44567	45333
47542	53800	53802	53803
53804	53805	53806	53807
53809	53810	73019	73028
75073	76026	82037	

31 locomotives on shed

At Bath we noted nine of the 11 Class '7F' 2-8-0s - only Nos 53801 and 53808 were missing. These engines (Nos 53800-53810) were designed by Fowler for the Somerset & Dorset Joint Railway and were taken into BR stock in 1930.

The buildings at Bath consisted of two separate engine sheds, the four-road ex-SDJR shed and the two-road ex-Midland shed.

LONDON: SATURDAY 20 DECEMBER - Class '5700' 0-6-0 pannier tank No 9770 was noted at Waterloo station. It had recently been re-allocated to Nine Elms (70A), but still carried an 82D shedplate (Westbury).

We visited London's first all-diesel locomotive depot, DEVONS ROAD (BOW). The only remaining sign of the steam era at this date was a partly intact water tower in the outer yard.

DEVONS ROAD (BOW) DEPOT

Diesel locomotives:
D2901 D2902 D2904 D2905 D2906 D8010 D8013 D8014 D8017 D8200 D8201 D8203 D8205

13 locomotives on shed

My only other visit to this depot had been on Saturday 23 February 1957 with the South Hants Locospotters Club (page 25). On that visit there had been 29 steam and one diesel shunter on shed.

Whenever visiting London with a party of enthusiasts which included Jim Lawrence, it always proved to be 'a bit mad'. Jim, apart from being a keen railway enthusiast, also had a mania for collecting or doing the unusual. One such pastime, in which we also participated, especially when travelling on crowded tube trains, was to count the number of men with bald heads! We used the word 'dome', and on this trip to London it was recorded that we noted no fewer than 163 domes! All very silly, but it did help to pass time and alleviate boredom when travelling underground.

On alighting from a crowded tube-train we would often leave a note on the seat, for example a piece of paper with the date and the number of 'domes' noted on that particular train. Passengers who found these notes after our departure must have been quite mystified!

THE PORTSMOUTH AREA DURING 1958

**FRATTON: SUNDAY
26 JANUARY**

FRATTON DEPOT

Steam locomotives:
30022	30039	30328	30357
30496	30545	30726	30729
30732	30856	31408	31637
31807	31809	31895	32139
32337	32349	32479	32495
32509	32548	32549	32640
32650	32661	32677	32694
76017	76059		

Diesel locomotive:
13011

31 locomotives on shed

Nos 30022/39/328/357 were Class 'M7' 0-4-4s. No 30328 was undergoing repair on the depot crane; it had all its wheels removed.

'Lord Nelson' Class 4-6-0 No 30856, *Lord St Vincent* had been employed the previous day to haul one of the football excursion trains to Wolverhampton. It probably took the train as far as Basingstoke and then returned to Portsmouth.

One of Dugald Drummond's long-lived classes was the 'M7' 0-4-4 tank design.

By 1958, having left school, my interests began to diversify. Although I remained interested in railways, other interests came to the fore, notably football (watching and playing), pop music and the cinema. As already mentioned, I was now employed in the printing industry, and reproduced below is an example of the front cover of the Portsmouth Football Club programme, which I regularly helped

R. ROBSON

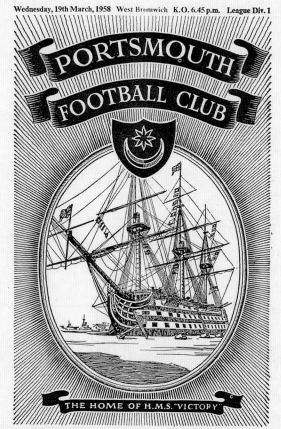

Near right The familiar Portsmouth FC programme cover depicting HMS *Victory*. At this time I was an apprentice at Grosvenor Press in Blackfriars Road, Southsea, printers of this programme - I helped to set up the pages in my capacity as a hot metal hand compositor.

Centre right The teams that lined up for the Pompey v WBA match at Fratton Park on Wednesday 19 March 1958. Pompey won 2-1 with goals by Johnny Gordon and Derek Dougan. The attendance was 24,731, kick-off 6.45 pm. Programme 3d.

Far right Of interest on the back page of the programme are the rail notice to IoW supporters and the 'Berg' ad - who would like a new house for £1,750 these days!

Above One of the WBA players (No 8) in this particular match was none other than the England Manager of the 1980s and the World Cup in 1990, Bobby Robson!

Going to the Cinema

CLASSIC, Commercial Road. — Today, Doris Day, James Cagney, "Love Me or Leave Me" (a), Colour and Cinemascope, 1.40, 5.10, 8.25. Gordon Harker, Marie Lohr, "Small Hotel" (u), 3.55, 7.15.

CRITERION, Gosport.—Today, Stanley Baker, "Sea Fury" (a) at 2.15, 5.25, 8.35. Ben Piazza, "A Dangerous Age" (a), at 3.55, 7.00. L.C.P. 7.00.

CURZON, Waterlooville. — William Holden, Sophia Loren, "The Key" (a), 4.20, 8.05. "The True Story of Lynn Stewart" (a), 2.45, 6.30. Open 2.30. L.C.P. 6.30.

EMPIRE, Havant. — Today, Marlon Brando, Montgomery Clift, "The Young Lions" (a), 4.25, 7.30. Sat. 1.20. Full supporting programme at 4.10, 7.15. Sat. 1.05.

ESSOLDO, Southsea.—Today, Elizabeth Taylor, Montgomery Clift in "Raintree County" (Tech.), 1.30, 4.35, 7.45. L.c.p. 7.30.

GAUMONT, Southsea. — Jerry Lewis in "Rock-a-Bye Baby" (u), daily 2.05, 5.15, 8.25. Jack Watling in "Links of Justice" (u), daily at 3.50, 7.10. Doors open 1.50 p.m. L.C.P. 7.05 p.m.

ODEON, North End. Phone 64047. Today, Virginia McKenna, Bill Travers, Yvonne Mitchell, "Passionate Summer" (a), Eastmancolour, 2.15, 5.30, 8.40, and William Sylvester, "Dublin Nightmare" (u), 4.05, 7.15.

ODEON, Southsea. Telephone 32163. Today, Virginia McKenna, Bill Travers in "Passionate Summer" (a), daily at 2.15, 5.25, 8.40, William Sylvester in "Dublin Nightmare" (u), daily at 4.00, 7.10. Doors open at 1.45.

ODEON, Cosham. Phone 76547. Virginia McKenna, Bill Travers, Yvonne Mitchell, "Passionate Summer" (a), 2.15, 5.25, 8.40, "Dublin Nightmare" (u). 4.00, 7.15.

ESSOLDO, Cosham.—Today, Elizabeth Taylor, Montgomery Clift in "Raintree County" Tech. 1.30, 4.35, 7.45. L.C.P. 7.30.

ESSOLDO, Kingston Cross. — Today, Rock Hudson, Jennifer Jones, "A Farewell to Arms" (a), 2.00, 4.50, 7.45.

ESSOLDO, Eastney. — Today, "Carve Her Name With Pride" Paul Scofield, 5.20, 8.10. "Person Unknown" 7.20.

FORUM, Gosport. — Today, Max Bygraves, in "A Cry From the Streets" (u), 1.56, 5.12, 8.28. "Golden Age of Comedy" (u), 3.56, 7.12. Doors 1.30 p.m. L.C.P. 6.50 p.m.

FORUM, Stamshaw Road. — Today, Dirk Bogarde in "A Tale of Two Cities" (u) at 2.0, 5.10, 8.15. Susan Shaw in "Diplomatic Corpse" (u), at 4.0, 7.5.

GAIETY. — 1.30. L.C.P. 7.0. Fred MacMurray in "Far Horizon" (u), 1.45, 5.10, 8.40, Tech. Fernando Lamas "Lost Treasure of the Amazon" (u), 3.35, 7.0, Tech.

GAUMONT, North End. Phone 62834. — Today, Jerry Lewis, "Rock-a-Bye Baby" (u) Technicolour, Vistavision, 2.00, 5.20, 8.35. Jack Watling, Sarah Lawson, "Links of Justice" (u), 3.55, 7.10. Doors 1.45. L.C.P. 7.05.

PALACE.—Tony Curtis, "The Square Jungle" (a), Dly at 2.25, 5.30, 8.45. John Agar, "Star in the Dust" (u), Tech, 3.50, 7.05.

REX, Fratton Road. —Today, "The Great Lover" (a), Fernandel, 5.40, 8.50, "Honour Among Thieves" 4.05, 7.15. Both Sub-titles.

RITZ, Gosport. — 1.30 p.m.; L.C.P. 7.30 p.m. - James Stewart, Kim Novak, "Vertigo" (a), 2.30, 5.20, 8.15, 8.20.

SAVOY (A.B.C.).—Today. Montgomery Clift, Elizabeth Taylor, Nigel Patrick, "Raintree County" (a), (Technicolour), 1.15, 4.30, 7.45.

SHAFTESBURY, Kingston Road. Today, Fred MacMurray, Charlton Heston in "Far Horizons" (u), 1.45, 5.05, 8.30. Fernando Lamas, "Lost Treasure of the Amazon" (u), 3.35, 6.55. L.C.P. 6.55.

TROXY, Dan Kelly in "The Valley of Death" 3.0, 5.55, 9.0, and Brandon Carol, "Hell Squad" at 1.40, 4.35, 7.35.

TIVOLI, Copnor. — Today. Max Bygraves, "A Cry from the Streets" (u), Mon. to Fri. 5.25, 8.24, Sat. 2.35, 5.25, 8.24. Will Rogers, Laurel and Hardy, "Golden Age of Comedy" (u), Mon. to Fri. 7.12, Sat. 4.15, 7.12.

VICTORIA (A.B.C.). — Today. Max Bygraves, "A Cry from the Streets" (u), 2.10, 5.20, 8.30. "Golden Age of Comedy" (u), 4.15, 7.15.

to set up for each home match. A particularly interesting match that I attended at Fratton Park that year was on 19 March and some of the details from the programme of that match are also reproduced.

One of our favourite haunts for pop music and dancing was at this date was the Savoy Ballroom, Southsea. Bands and groups ranged from rock 'n' roll to Ken Mackintosh and his Orchestra. In

Above Going to the cinema was another pastime which we always enjoyed. In this 1958 advertisement, Portsmouth citizens could choose from no fewer than 24 cinemas in their area - nowadays there are only three! *Reproduced by kind permission of The News, formerly The Evening News, Portsmouth*

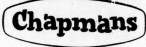
FOOTBALL LEAGUE — DIVISION I

	P	W	D	L	F	A	Pts			P	W	D	L	F	A	Pts
Wolverhampton	33	23	6	4	85	39	52		Bolton	34	13	7	14	57	71	33
Preston N.E.	33	20	5	8	82	44	45		Arsenal	33	14	4	15	62	68	32
West Brom. A.	33	16	12	5	79	53	44		Everton	33	10	11	12	50	58	31
Luton Town	34	17	5	12	60	47	39		Birmingham	34	10	10	14	57	77	30
Manchester City	34	17	4	13	86	87	38		Aston Villa	33	11	5	17	56	70	27
Manchester U.	31	15	7	9	74	55	37		Portsmouth	32	10	6	16	55	62	26
Tottenham	34	15	7	12	75	70	37		Newcastle	32	10	5	17	55	61	25
Blackpool	33	15	6	12	65	53	36		Leicester City	34	10	5	19	73	91	25
Nottingham F.	34	15	5	14	65	54	35		Sheffield Wed.	34	9	6	19	61	81	24
Burnley	33	16	3	14	64	63	35		Leeds United	33	9	6	18	41	58	24
Chelsea	34	13	7	14	74	72	33		Sunderland	34	7	10	17	42	84	24

NOTICE TO ISLE OF WIGHT SUPPORTERS

Supporters returning to the Isle of Wight after the game this evening will be able to travel from Fratton Station direct to the Harbour Station. Special trains will leave Fratton Station at 8.36 p.m. and 8.41 p.m. to connect with the last boat to Ryde.

Fratton shed was visited on the date of the WBA match and Class 'E4' 0-6-2 tank No 32479 was in the yard. *David Copus*

1958 you could get this entertainment from 7.30 pm until midnight for just 4 shillings!

FRATTON: SATURDAY 14 JUNE - This early summer Saturday saw no fewer than six 'Hall' Class 4-6-0s from the Western Region arrive at the station, one of

these being the Reading to Portsmouth ordinary service on which No 7927 *Willington Hall* was used. Numbers and names noted were 4917 *Crosswood Hall*, 4938 *Liddington Hall*, 5914 *Ripon Hall* (on a nine-carriage excursion from Gloucester), 5957 *Hutton Hall*, and 6930 *Aldersey Hall*.

Two 'Battle of Britain' 4-6-2s, Nos 34066 *Spitfire* and 34077 603 *Squadron*, were noted in the depot yard, having brought excursions

JUNE 1958 - 'HAMPSHIRE' DIESELS ARRIVE ON THE SCENE . . .

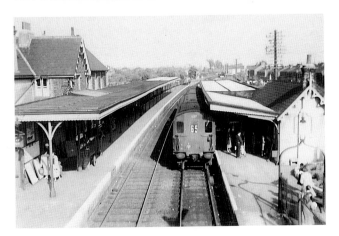

Below left One of the newly introduced 'Hampshire' diesel units is seen at Cosham station forming a Portsmouth Harbour to Salisbury train. The date is June 1958 and the unit No is 1107. *Jack Stillwell*

'Hampshire' diesel electric services began on Monday 9 June 1958 with two-car and three-car sets in green livery. Reproduced here is a map of the area covered, together with some fares at this date.

MAP OF AREA SERVED BY DIESEL-ELECTRIC TRAINS

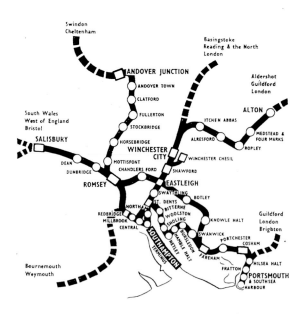

CHEAP DAY TICKETS TO PORTSMOUTH AND SOUTHSEA DAILY BY ALL TRAINS	1st Class	2nd Class
Eastleigh	7/6	5/-
Fareham	3/9	2/6
Southampton Central	8/-	5/4
Southampton Terminus	8/-	5/4
Winchester City	9/9	6/6

DAY EXCURSIONS TO PORTSMOUTH AND SOUTHSEA BY SPECIFIED TRAINS ON MONDAYS TO SATURDAYS	1st Class	2nd Class
Andover Junction	15/6	10/3
Andover Town	15/6	10/3

DAY EXCURSIONS TO PORTSMOUTH AND SOUTHSEA BY SPECIFIED TRAINS DAILY	1st Class	2nd Class
Romsey	10/3	6/9
Salisbury	15/6	10/3

CHEAP TICKETS TO PORTSMOUTH AND SOUTHSEA DAILY BY ALL TRAINS AFTER 9.30 a.m.	1st Class	2nd Class
Eastleigh	6/2	4/1
Fareham	3/-	2/-
Romsey	8/9	5/10
Southampton Central	7/2	4/9
Southampton Terminus	7/2	4/9
Winchester City	8/3	5/6

CHEAP DAY TICKETS TO SOUTHAMPTON CENTRAL DAILY BY ALL TRAINS	1st Class	2nd Class
Alton	7/11	5/3
Eastleigh	2/-	1/4
Fareham	4/11	3/3
Romsey	3/-	2/-
Salisbury	7/9	5/2

CHEAP TICKETS TO SOUTHAMPTON CENTRAL DAILY BY ALL TRAINS AFTER 9.30 a.m.	1st Class	2nd Class
Portsmouth and Southsea	7/2	4/9

(The fares shown above are liable to alteration).

4

from the London area into Bognor Regis and then travelled light to Fratton shed for coaling-up and water before returning later in the day to pick up the return excursions. What is of particular note is that *Spitfire* was the locomotive involved in the Lewisham rail disaster in December 1957; as mentioned above (page 76), it was seen at Bricklayers Arms depot (73B) on 9 February where it was waiting pending a decision on its future use after being badly damaged in the disaster. All those who were at Bricklayers Arms four months previously, and saw the badly damaged locomotive, thought that it would almost certainly be scrapped - we were to be proved wrong!

Apart from train-spotting from Fratton station footbridge, we often helped passengers to carry their cases up the stairs from platforms 2 and 3 and then down the stairs to platform 1. This practice was most frequent during summer Saturdays when holidaymakers were arriving, some of them having come from the West Country and needing to 'change at Fratton' for connection to the Brighton and Victoria lines. It was quite

common to be handed a sixpence or a shilling tip for our services. I don't think the station staff objected to us helping, as it saved them having to carry or trolley luggage across the main lines at the Portsmouth end of the platforms.

FRATTON: JULY - This month saw two Fratton 'T9' 4-4-0s, Nos 30726 and 30729, re-allocated, 30726 going to Exmouth Junction and 30729 to Bournemouth. This left only one 'T9' at Fratton shed, No 30732. New allocations were Class 'M7' 0-4-4 tank No 30356 from Eastleigh, Class 'A1X' 0-6-0 tank No 32678 from St Leonards (74E) and Class 'G6' 0-6-0 tank No 30349 on loan from Guildford. One of the two Fratton-allocated Class 'K' 2-6-0s, No 32337, returned from Ashford Works, whilst 'E4' 0-6-2 tank No 32479 was re-shedded to Brighton.

A visit was made to Hayling Island. I changed at Havant to catch the branch-line train hauled by Class 'A1X' 0-6-0 tank No 32677. There were water and coal facilities in the bay platform at Havant station. The return fare from Fratton to Hayling Island was 2/10d.

SUMMER OF '58 - Some interesting notings in Portsmouth.

'West Country' No 34095 *Brentor* arrived with an excursion that it had taken over at Kensington Olympia. Two DMU excursions arrived, one from Cheshunt and one from Southend. Leicester (Midland)-shedded Standard Class '5' 4-6-0 No 73140 travelled via the Willesden Junction, Staines and Guildford route to Portsmouth Harbour station, having come from Hinckley.

Other notings during August and September were Standard Class '5' 4-6-0 No 73035 on the 8.50 am to Wolverhampton (16 August) and 'Hall' Class 4-6-0s Nos 4918 *Dartington Hall*, 5906 *Lawton Hall*, 5915 *Trentham Hall*, 5973 *Rolleston Hall*, 5993 *Kirby Hall*, 6922 *Burton Hall*, and 6924 *Grantley Hall*. Three 'Schools' Class 4-4-0s came in, Nos 30900 *Eton*, 30902 *Wellington* and 30905 *Tonbridge*. 'Lord Nelson' 4-6-0 No 30850 *Lord Nelson* was an early September visitor. Two ex-Great Central carriages in brown livery found their way to sidings adjacent to Fratton West signal box; their numbers were E61596E and E63699E.

Railway enthusiasts at Fratton often had items printed in *Trains Illustrated* magazine. A paragraph appeared in 1958 under 'Motive Power Miscellany', Southern Region, Western Section:

Among numerous WR arrivals at Portsmouth during the month, the most outstanding was 'Manor' No 7820 (83D) on July 9. For SR information we are indebted to Messrs D. Wood, M. C. Myhill, M. Hedges, A. H. Martin, R. Smart, D. P. Clegg, M. H. Green, P. K. Tunks, D. F. Glenn, B. Young, E. C. Rooke, M. Harvey, C. Brooks, S. Tracey.

(Information by kind permission of Ian Allan)

Class 'Q' 0-6-0 No 30531 simmers quietly in Fratton shed yard in 1958.

Left Always a favourite tank engine was Class 'E1' 0-6-0 No 32694. Introduced in 1874 and at this date still working daily, it was employed on the goods train from Fratton sidings to the Dockyard, which would usually consist of about six assorted wagons and vans. No 32694 is seen here in unlined black livery and in excellent condition in Fratton shed yard.

Below Standard Class '4' 2-6-0 No 76011 (71A) in Fratton yard. One of my friends, David Bodenham, is seen in the cab.

SATURDAY 6 DECEMBER -

'C2X' 0-6-0 No 32548 worked the Cardiff train as far as Fareham. 'T9' No 30120, in spotless condition, was observed. Class 'U' 2-6-0 No 31795 brought in a football excursion for the Portsmouth v Arsenal Division One match, which I attended; the crowd was 33,321, Pompey lost 0-1 and my team were relegated at the end of the 1958-9 season!

WEDNESDAY 17 DECEMBER -

On this day and frequently during 1958, Reading-allocated 'Hall' No 4995 *Easton Hall* was employed on the daily Reading to Portsmouth train. 'Schools' 4-4-0 No 30902 *Wellington* was employed on a Christmas parcels train. 'T9' 4-4-0 No 30732 worked tender-first from platform 1 at Portsmouth & Southsea (Low Level) at 12.15 pm on the Plymouth train, taking it as far as Fareham.

THE SOUTHERN REGION RAILROVER

LONDON

SUNDAY 4 JANUARY

I went on this trip with local railway enthusiasts Eddie Rooke, David Copus, Charlie Best, David Bodenham, Frank Allen, Mike Dooley and Trevor Robson. The return fare was 15/6d.

It was 6 am exactly as I and the travelling party gathered outside Fratton station entrance - it was extremely cold and foggy, and snow had been forecast for the Hampshire area. We were to have taken the first train to Waterloo, the 6.08 am stopping at all stations and halts, but engineering work was in progress between Fratton and Havant, so a double-decker bus was laid on to take passengers to the latter point. The bus departed at 6.20 am and travelled via Goldsmith Avenue, Eastern Road and Havant Road to Havant station entrance - as on a previous trip, the guard blew his whistle to start the bus off from Fratton!

On arrival at Havant we transferred to a ten-carriage electric unit train which consisted of five two-carriage sets (2-BILs). Eventual departure was at 7 am. Our party occupied two complete compartments of non-corridor stock, and we settled down for games of cards, playing for money. The journey from Havant was slow, our window had become iced up and it was impossible to see through it. We ground to a halt near Rowlands Castle station and when we opened the window we saw snow drifts all around us; it was snowing heavily and visibility was very poor. We were stationary

for nearly 15 minutes, and found out from someone further along the train that the electric unit had failed due to ice and snow on the conductor rail and that a steam locomotive was being summoned from Fratton shed to haul us.

At 7.30 am Billinton-designed Class 'K' 2-6-0 engine No 32349 (70F) appeared on the scene, coupled up to the ten-carriage electric train and slowly moved off. The 'K' was making heavy work of its load which was about 375 tons; it travelled tender-first at a steady 25 to 30 mph in the direction of Guildford. This was indeed an experience for railway enthusiasts on this trip; it was the first time ever that any of our party had been steam-hauled on the direct Portsmouth to Waterloo line, and for it to be in this manner was exceptional to say the least! The 'K' Class 2-6-0s' normal duties consisted of light freight and carriage workings, but nevertheless No 32349 became a 'local hero' on this trip, eventually bringing our train into Guildford.

We watched the engine being taken off at the station and saw it travel to the adjacent engine shed (70C) for coaling-up and water. The snowbound area was now behind us, but the weather was bitterly cold with flurries of light snow still falling. The ten-carriage electric unit train then continued under its own power to Waterloo, arriving at 10.10 am, the 90-minute journey having taken a total of 3 hours and 50 minutes!

Card games had been played throughout the journey and, on approaching Waterloo, Charlie Best was seen frantically totalling up his cash remains. He had lost

BETWEEN FRATTON AND WATERLOO

Steam locomotives:
30023 30124 30246 30513
30794 30795 30905 31722
35016 35018 73116 73117

heavily, but some of us 'chipped in' to help him out of his embarrassing position - enough to pay his tube train fares, anyway!

The first depot visited was CAMDEN (1B) - there were 49 on shed, including No 71000 *Duke of Gloucester*, the only multi-cylinder design on British Railways.

Our second depot of the visit was STRATFORD (East London) and our route was via Liverpool Street. We had a permit to visit this depot which we handed to the gateman at 11.30 am. We linked up with others parties and an official guide took us round the depot and yards. This was the *largest locomotive depot on British Railways*, and had, at one time, about 400 locomotives in its allocation!

Stratford consisted of two through sheds, one of 12 roads which was over 100 yards long, and a smaller one of six roads.

Stratford depot (30A) was visited for the first time on this trip. We noted 15 of these Class 'B1' 4-6-0s on shed, two of which were named.

STRATFORD DEPOT

Steam locomotives:

31	32	36	43107	47282	47306	47311	61000	61004	61059	61104	61111	61119
61171	61260	61335	61336	61362	61371	61375	61378	61399	61547	61549	61561	61564
61573	61576	61655	61658	61661	61668	61815	61863	61963	61981	62013	62014	62053
62066	62518	62534	62543	62545	62566	62571	62572	62582	62588	62610	62615	63619
63637	63746	63872	64641	64645	64649	64652	64655	64657	64663	64668	64669	64672
64675	64676	64680	64681	64685	64688	64689	64694	64697	64699	64708	64765	64766
64767	64768	64773	64781	64783	64784	64787	64788	64805	64873	64874	64965	64972
65361	65390	65438	65440	65441	65444	65449	65463	65464	65467	65476	65525	65536
65545	65546	65555	65561	65563	67708	67712	67715	67718	67723	67724	67725	67726
67727	67729	67733	67735	67737	68513	68526	68529	68538	68549	68563	68575	68577
68578	68612	68613	68618	68619	68625	68630	68632	68633	68636	68639	68644	68647
68648	68649	68650	68652	68655	68658	68659	68660	68663	68744	69602	69608	69610
69611	69614	69615	69616	69619	69623	69627	69628	69630	69639	69641	69651	69652
69656	69658	69659	69660	69662	69667	69676	69685	69687	69691	69696	69703	69705
69710	69711	69713	69714	69715	69716	69717	69718	69719	69721	69723	69732	70005
70009	70034	80077	90001	90023	90062	90244	90484	90498	90508	90522	90551	90559
90660	90709											

Diesel locomotives:

D200	D202	D203	D204	11100	11122	11123	11131	11132	11133	11134	11505	12064
12103	12105	12106	12127	12130	12133	12136	D2208	D2210	D2214	D2957	D2958	13219
D3300	13334	D3442	D3444	D3460	D3464	D3476	D3497	D3498	D3499	D3501	D3502	D3608
D3635	D3681	D3682	D3684	15214	D5504	D5510	D5511	D5513	D8400	D8401	D8402	D8403
D8404	D8405	D8406	D8407	D8408								

267 locomotives on shed

Nos 31/2/6 were Class 'J66' 0-6-0 tank locomotives, introduced in 1886 to a Holden (Great Eastern) design. Used as Departmental stock and allocated to the depot works. Former BR numbers were 68382 (31), 68370 (32) and 68378 (36).

There was also a separate two-road shed used by Stratford Works service locomotives. The shed was very widespread and there were extensive sidings in the area. It certainly took us considerable time to complete!

We then travelled from Stratford station to Liverpool Street and walked to Broad Street where we caught an electric train to Willesden Junction.

On arrival at Willesden Junction we walked to Old Oak Common depot, passing on the way the entrance of Willesden depot. Old Oak was visited first as we had a permit with a specified time typed on it; we were behind

We purchased single tickets between Broad Street and Willesden Junction. The fare was 10d.

schedule, but the gateman checked our permit and let us proceed.

OLD OAK COMMON (81A) - of the 127 on shed, surprisingly ten were 'King' Class 4-6-0s: Nos 6003,

6007, 6009, 6010, 6011, 6012, 6019, 6020, 6023 and 6026.

WILLESDEN DEPOT (1A) - there were 141 on shed but this included 17 diesels, a sure sign that dieselisation was increasing.

Our method of transport between Willesden and our next depot, Cricklewood, was a trolleybus. We alighted at the depot entrance in the North Circular Road.

CRICKLEWOOD DEPOT (14A) - of the 78 engines on shed, 13 were Class '9F' 2-10-0s, Nos 92023, 92027, 92050, 92052, 92055, 92080, 92107, 92108,

92110, 92111, 92130, 92154 and 92158.

KENTISH TOWN DEPOT (14B) - there were 75 on shed including from the 'old order' seven Class '2P' 4-4-0s, Nos 40421, 40511, 40548, 40550, 40567, 40580 and 40583, 'Compound' 4-4-0 No 41100 and, from the modern era, 'Britannia' Class 4-6-2s Nos 70014 *Iron Duke* and 70021 *Morning Star*.

The next depot of the visit was Devons Road (Bow). It was getting late and darkness was upon us as we made our way to Devons Road via Kentish Town, Liverpool Street and Bromley (District line). We walked from Bromley station to the depot.

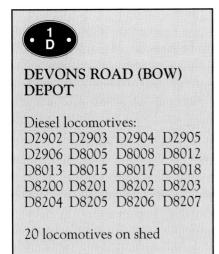

DEVONS ROAD (BOW) DEPOT

Diesel locomotives:
D2902 D2903 D2904 D2905
D2906 D8005 D8008 D8012
D8013 D8015 D8017 D8018
D8200 D8201 D8202 D8203
D8204 D8205 D8206 D8207

20 locomotives on shed

On a previous visit (February 1957, page 25) 29 steam and one diesel had been noted - now it was a total 'diesel only' shed.

On leaving Devons Road we continued via the District line to West Ham for our eighth and final visit of the day, Plaistow.

On alighting at West Ham we walked through an area which was dominated by blocks of high-rise flats. We had no permit to visit Plaistow depot so it was decided that our party of eight should split up on entering the depot. This we did, half of us tackling one side

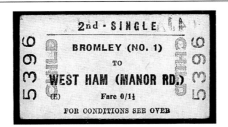

Ticket used between Bromley and West Ham. Note the fare of 1¹/₂d (half).

whilst the others concentrated on the opposite side. Using this method we could rely on noting all or most of the engines on shed - if one half did get stopped by an official, the remainder of the party would compare lists and then make up a total between them. This procedure was used whenever the occasion demanded, especially after darkness had fallen as on this visit. We did manage to get round without being questioned and all the engines on shed were noted.

PLAISTOW DEPOT - there were 32 on shed which included eight

The child single used for the journey from West Ham. The fare was 7d.

Standard Class '4' 2-6-4 tanks, Nos 80069, 80072, 80074, 80096, 80099, 80100, 80102 and 80131.

Leaving the depot we travelled via Liverpool Street to Charing Cross. Our eventful day ended by walking across Hungerford Bridge which spans the River Thames, entering Waterloo station and catching the electric unit train home to Portsmouth. The day would be best remembered by the events on the forward journey, and my first ever visit to Stratford depot noting no fewer than 267 locomotives on shed.

ACCRINGTON FOOTBALL EXCURSION

FRIDAY 23 AND SATURDAY 24 JANUARY

I went on this Refreshment Car Excursion with local railway enthusiasts Tony Ingram ('Inky') and Ian Gray, as well as numerous other local train-spotters. This 'Special' was laid on to take Portsmouth Football Club supporters, team and officials to the Lancashire town of Accrington for a Third Round FA Cup match.

A very large gathering of Pompey supporters were on our departure platform at Portsmouth Harbour. They were in fine voice and the Pompey banner with masses of blue and white scarves were to be seen. Portsmouth, at this date, were struggling at the wrong end of the First Division, whilst Accrington Stanley (as they were known) were an average Third Division side. The return fare was 37/6d.

The excursion carriages were slowly backed into the station at

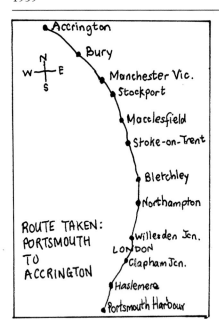

ROUTE TAKEN: PORTSMOUTH TO ACCRINGTON

NORTHAMPTON, STOKE-ON-TRENT, MACCLESFIELD AND STOCKPORT AREAS

Steam locomotives:

42118	42304	42343	42357
42443	42482	42600	42657
42713	42942	44093	44310
44507	44741	45034	45181
45242	45257	45374	45387
45404	45604	45631	45733
46221	46430	47601	47658
48154	48188	48621	48744
49147	49191	67751	90372
90609	90649		

MANCHESTER (VICTORIA), BURY, ACCRINGTON AND LOWER DARWEN AREAS

Steam locomotives:

40120	40162	40183	40631
41287	42153	42288	42295
42311	42433	42456	42474
42475	42481	42483	42547
42548	42559	42643	42714
42715	42819	42829	43031
44311	44479	44696	44889
45227	45418	46484	46486
47201	47475	47493	47579
49624	50647	52108	52271
75019	76081	76084	80044
80046	84011	90205	90564
90718			

Nos 52108/271 were Class '3F' 0-6-0 locomotives introduced in 1889 and still in working order - both were noted in steam in their 70th year! Also of note was Class '2P' 2-4-2 tank engine No 50647, also 70 years old!

11.05 pm on Friday night by Fratton-allocated Class 'C2X' 0-6-0 No 32550. At the front of the train was the locomotive which was to haul us as far as Willesden Junction, 'West Country' 4-6-2 No 34007 *Wadebridge*.

The excursion departed on time at 11.26 pm, the 'C2X' being used as a 'banker' out of the station. Our route was via Havant, Haslemere, Wimbledon and Clapham Junction to Willesden Junction, and we passed through a very industrial scene as we approached Willesden, with much evidence of freight trains in sidings loading and unloading their goods. Only five steam engines were noted between Clapham Junction and Willesden Junction: Nos 9705, 33002, 34065, 45142 and 48534. Two diesels were also noted: D8007 and D8010.

Wadebridge came off at Willesden Junction and we were then steam-hauled by 'Black Five' 4-6-0 No 45064 of Willesden shed. Departure time was 1.30 am and up to this point we had had no sleep as locomotive activity along our route had kept us occupied.

The first signs of daylight were beginning to show as we

approached the Stoke area. Our journey was amidst an industrial background of factories, blast furnaces, gas works and countless chimneys giving out their grey waste against the pale morning sky. We had very little chance of any sustained periods of sleep - in

fact, I did not sleep at all! The general activity in sidings and stations prevented that.

On arrival at Manchester (Victoria) Class '3' 2-6-2 tank No 40129 was attached to the front of 'Black Five' No 45064, and then piloted the excursion to Accrington.

It was nearly 8.30 am when the excursion train pulled into Accrington station. On our arrival we purchased half fare return tickets to Bolton. The Accrington Football Club Supporters Club had come to meet the Portsmouth supporters at the railway station and they had kindly laid on breakfasts for us after our long overnight journey. Many accepted this generous offer, but we turned it down as we had already had sandwiches and a drink on the train on the way. Once again the Pompey supporters were in good voice and the Pompey banner was proudly displayed on the station platform.

Although we did not send for any permits to visit locomotive depots in the area, we had planned to visit three depots, Lower Darwen (24D), Bolton (26C) and finally Accrington (24A) before walking to Peel Park to see the football match, due to kick off at 3 pm.

A local train arrived at the station platform on which we were standing. I enquired of the station ticket collector whether it went to Lower Darwen. He said 'Yes' and then commenced reading out on the microphone in a Lancastrian accent, which we could only partially make out, all the names of the stations the train would be calling at. We assumed that we were on the correct train although we were not really sure. Anyway, by now it had started to pull away from the station!

On approaching Lower Darwen station the train did not slow down - in fact, it did not stop at Lower Darwen! The ticket collector at Accrington was right in telling us that the train went to Lower Darwen, but we had not asked if it stopped there!

We continued to Bolton (Trinity Street) station, and it was decided that we would remain on board as the train was going to Manchester. As there were numerous steam locomotives noted between Accrington and Bolton we thought it best to note engine numbers from the train rather than visit depots and be turned away for having no permits.

A 'flit' round the Blackburn, Bolton and Manchester areas was made, all this being achieved with one half fare return ticket from Accrington to Bolton costing about 2 shillings. Steam haulage between Manchester (Victoria) and Bolton (Trinity Street) was by Standard Class '4' 4-6-0 locomotive No 75018 and between Manchester and Blackburn by Class '6P5F' 2-6-0 No 42760.

Returning to Accrington station at about 2.50 pm, we walked to Peel Park very briskly but carefully, as a layer of snow had covered the area.

The teams had just kicked off as we entered the ground, and there was a distinct possibility that the match could be abandoned, but it continued and the final result was a 0-0 draw.

I had been a Portsmouth Football Club supporter since the early 1950s and followed their fortunes at most home games. This excursion gave us a chance to visit one of the smaller Third Division teams and at the same time combine it with the noting of some very interesting steam locomotives, many of them being local to the Lancashire area only.

The Portsmouth team was: Brown; McGhee, Gunter; Carter, Hayward, Dickinson; P. Harris, Weddle, Saunders, H. Harris, Newman. The attendance was 12,590.

BOLTON, BLACKBURN AND MANCHESTER AREAS

Steam locomotives:

40015	40066	40077	42147
42287	42289	42297	42433
42465	42547	42565	42619
42630	42634	42644	42652
42653	42654	42660	42703
42706	42719	42753	42785
42828	42860	42861	42937
44460	44479	44696	44770
44803	44863	44887	44926
44933	44950	44982	44987
45068	45077	45078	45116
45201	45232	45233	45336
45450	45567	45661	45705
46104	46485	48491	48895
49618	49662	49674	63582
73127	75018	75049	78044
90116	90212	90277	90324
90470	90641		

After the match we had a hot meal (a quick visit to a fish and chip shop), then the return excursion departed from Accrington at 5.27 pm. At this point we were very tired and looking forward to some much-needed sleep. The excursion arrived at Fratton station at 3.45 am Sunday.

GOSPORT CENTENARY

SUNDAY 25 JANUARY

I did not get to sleep until 4.15 am on my return from Accrington, but 5 hours later I awoke, had breakfast and then paid a brief visit to Fratton station. Some engines noted were Nos 30349, 30547 and 42066.

I returned home for a roast Sunday lunch, after which I visited Gosport with Bill Jenkins and several other local train-spotters in the early afternoon. We travelled by train from Fratton to Portsmouth Harbour where we alighted and caught the ferry across the harbour to Gosport. We walked from the pontoon to the location of the former Gosport terminus station in Spring Garden Lane, this taking us just over 10 minutes.

The reason for our visit was to see a special train that was being run to celebrate the centenary of the opening of the direct line between London and Portsmouth. The special, which was the first passenger train to visit Gosport for almost six years, left London (Victoria) and travelled via Effingham Junction and Woking to Godalming. A Class '0395' 0-6-0 freight locomotive (built in the early 1880s) was used to haul the special from London to Guildford, where it came off; Class '700' 0-6-0 locomotive No 30350, one of the so-called 'Black Motors', then took over for the remainder of the journey to Gosport, travelling via Havant, Cosham and Fareham.

Although this centenary train ran to celebrate the opening of the direct line between London and Portsmouth, it was never intended to run the train actually to Portsmouth. The train was promoted for railway enthusiasts and naturally the Gosport to Fareham line, having been closed to passengers for so long, was of much more interest to them. In fact, Gosport had a railway before Portsmouth - so if you had a centenary train it would be run to Gosport.

The new line, which made the direct journey possible by linking Godalming and Havant, was first used on 24 January 1859, so the centenary train missing the actual opening by just one day.

HUNDREDS of people crowded Gosport railway station yesterday for the memory-provoking visit of the first passenger train for almost six years.

They were crammed on the platform, thronged the level crossing gates, and packed on the footbridge. They overspilled on to the track and the train driver was instructed to make the last stage of the journey with caution.

There were similar scenes at Fareham and Fort Brockhurst Stations, as the train, run by two railway enthusiasts to celebrate the centenary of the opening of the direct line between London and Portsmouth, made its halting way from Victoria to the borough.

The train, comprising seven coaches, with some 220 persons aboard, left London towed by an Adams class goods engine, built about 1880, but at Guildford this was replaced by Drummond class engine of 1897.

Frozen points caused further delays, and from Fareham, where the train arrived 35 minutes late there were enforced stops as the fireman alighted, opened the series of level crossing gates, saw the train through and then boarded it again.

A series of official welcomes were given the passengers en route. The first was by the Mayor and Mayoress of Godalming (Coun. and Mrs. B. F. Grillo) at Godalming old terminus, where a passenger train had not run since 1897.

At Petersfield several hundred people—many of them in Victorian costume—lined the two platforms and footbridge to await the arrival of the train.

Then came the news of a signal failure at Farncombe, and, that the train would be an hour late.

Almost everyone went home to lunch, and then the train rumbled in at 1.10 p.m. — 20 minutes before it was expected— and there was only a handful of people to see it through.

Scores of others went back to the station at 1.30 p.m. only to find that the train had gone.

HUSTLE AT HAVANT

In the bustle at Havant Station the Chairman of the Havant and Waterloo Urban Council (Col. Oliver Jones and Mrs. Jones were unable to find Mr. G. R. Lockie, of Upper Norwood, who, with Mr. H. C. Grenside, of Hindhead, arranged the "Centenarian."

The centenary special puffed into the station more than half an hour behind schedule and the planned five-minute stop was reduced to just over a minute.

In that time Col. and Mrs. Jones boarded the third Pullman coach in which Mr. Lockie was expected to be travelling, but, surrounded by the railway enthusiasts who travelled on the train and those who had flocked to the station to meet it, it was difficult for them to search for anyone or be found themselves.

"It was disappointing," commented Mrs. Jones, "but at least we tried. It was quite an historic event really. The Pullman looked even more comfortable than those in use today."

Col. and Mrs. Jones were among some 200 people who thronged the down platform at Havant Station.

They were received by Havant's Stationmaster (Mr. R. Edwards) and warned of the delay.

At vantage points along the line through Havant and Bedhampton other enthusiasts waited through the lunch hour for a glimpse of the special.

JOINED BY LORD MAYOR

At Cosham the Lord-Mayor and Lady Mayoress of Portsmouth (Coun. and Mrs. A. L. Blake) joined the train.

On arrival at Fareham, the Chairman of the Urban District Council (Mr. A. G. Boniface) and Mrs. Boniface gave the welcome, and with the Mayor and Mayoress of Gosport (Ald. and Mrs. P. D. Blanch) travelled on to Gosport, where the Mayor entertained the civic heads and organizers of the journey at the Town Hall.

To each he presented a copy of the town guide and a reproduction of a photograph of Queen Victoria arriving at Gosport on October 14, 1844.

A number of the passengers, like the driver and fireman, wore costumes of the mid-Victorian period, and this was a particularly nostalgic touch for 86-year-old Mr. Walter Linney, of 8, St Andrew's Road, Gosport, who saw the train at the bomb scarred Gosport station.

He worked on the railway for 50 years, and was a driver on the Gosport, Fareham and Alton line for 35 years.

He was the fireman on the engine which hauled the train carrying Queen Victoria's coffin from Royal Clarence Yard to Fareham in 1901.

Mr Albert Harman was one of the passengers on the train.

Left 'Centenary Train's Struggle Through The Freeze' was the headline for this article, which appeared in the *Evening News* on 26 January 1959.

Below left The centenary train arriving at Fareham hauled by Class '700' 0-6-0 locomotive No 30350. Introduced in 1897, this Drummond-designed locomotive had at this date been in active service for 60 years and had, like many others, survived two World Wars. Its depot of allocation was Guildford (70C), the station from which it took over the train. The Lord Mayor of Portsmouth (Cllr A. L. Blake) and the Mayor of Gosport (Ald P. D. Blanch) met some of the Victorian-costumed passengers when the centenary train arrived at Gosport.

Article and photographs by courtesy of The News, Portsmouth (formerly Evening News)

Above The disused Gosport railway station. This ornate and classical station, which included a superb Tuscan colonnade in stone, was designed by architect Sir William Tite, better known for his design of the Royal Exchange in London. David Nicholson built this elaborate station for the sum of £10,980 in 1842, and it was in use for six years before Portsmouth's first station was opened. Queen Victoria used the station quite often *en route* to her Isle of Wight home at Osborne House. Its run-down state at the time of my visit was attributed to continued vandalism after being bombed during the Second World War. I sketched this scene at about the same time as the locomotive depot drawing.

Above right The remains of the locomotive depot at Gosport. This was the scene, as sketched by myself, several months after the visit.

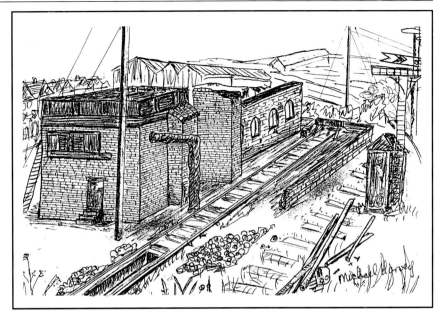

PLYMOUTH, NEWTON ABBOT AND EXETER

SUNDAY 19 JULY

This Sunday excursion from Portsmouth Harbour station was to be my second visit to the Plymouth, Exeter and Newton Abbot depots, as I had travelled on the corresponding excursion of the previous year (20 July 1958, page 63). The return fare was 12/10^{1}/2d (half fare). I travelled with Eddie Rooke, David Copus, Frank Allen, Terry Hunt, Timothy Julnes, Mike Dooley, Mike Chapman and Michael Ashcroft.

The excursion departed on time at 9.13 am. We were steam-hauled to Salisbury by Standard Class '4' 2-6-0 locomotive No 76005 (72B), our route being via Southampton Central. On arrival at Salisbury the Class '4' came off and we were then steam-hauled through to our destination, Plymouth (North Road), by 'Battle of Britain' 4-6-2

BETWEEN PORTSMOUTH AND PLYMOUTH (BOTH DIRECTIONS)

Steam locomotives:

1005	1011	1023	4179
4592	4636	5019	5069
5080	5153	5185	5976
6016	7813	30025	30129
30452	30522	30670	30824
30953	31614	31621	31791
31833	31836	31840	31849
31903	34020	34030	34035
34036	34053	34054	34056
34063	34069	34090	34104
35023	41307	48436	73089
76029			

Diesel locomotives:
DS49 DS1169 D3512 D3513 D3520 D3521 D3522 15230 15236

Nos DS49 and DS1169 were both 0-4-0 service types used for engineering works.

DS1169 was built in 1946 by the Bristol Aeroplane Company. Later purchased by BR, it was formerly at Folkestone Warren. Its weight was only 7^{1}/4 tons.

Both locos were noted on passing Broad Clyst Engineers Depot.

One of the party who came on this trip was Frank Allen. He is seen here at Eastleigh.

PLYMOUTH AND NEWTON ABBOT VIA TOTNES

Steam locomotives:
4561	4928	4978	5148
6002	6420	6871	7333

No 34049 *Anti Aircraft Command.*

Two steam locomotives noted (not in the list on page 89) were Class 'T9' 4-4-0 No 30702 on shed at Okehampton, a sub-depot of Exmouth Junction, and DS3152, a Class 'G6' 0-6-0 tank, introduced in 1894, which was noted at Meldon Quarry. Its former BR number was 30272.

On our arrival at North Road

station we walked to the main Western Region shed, LAIRA (PLYMOUTH) (83D), where 76 locomotives were on shed including 17 diesels (only two were shunters, an early indication of the decline of steam power in this area). Of note was Class '5700' 0-6-0 pannier tank No 6771 which was in use as a stationary boiler in the depot roundhouse. It had been

deleted from the official lists of working engines at this date.

We then walked to the former Southern Region shed, PLYMOUTH (FRIARY) (83H). This shed contained only 19 locomotives, of which four were Bulleid 'Pacifics'.

Leaving the depot, we walked to North Road station where we caught a train to Newton Abbot.

We entered NEWTON ABBOT depot (83A) by the unofficial route, via the end of the station platform, as on the previous visit. The depot was still virtually 100 per cent steam, 77 being on shed with one solitary 0-6-0 diesel shunter. Steam locomotives included seven 'Castle' Class 4-6-0s (including No 7029 *Clun Castle*), three 'Manor' 4-6-0s, four '9F' 2-10-0s and Bulleid 'Pacific' No 34033 *Chard*. In the Works were Nos 2881, 3677, 4256, 8409 and D3519.

We were then steam-hauled to Exeter St David's, travelling via

---

(72 A)   EXMOUTH JUNCTION DEPOT

Steam locomotives:

30023	30024	30027	30044	30045	30182	30232	30317	30323	30327	30328	30374	30451
30582	30583	30667	30669	30676	30691	30717	30718	30841	30842	30845	30846	30950
30953	30955	30956	30957	31626	31832	31834	31836	31841	31843	31844	31846	32697
34006	34011	34015	34034	34047	34057	34061	34074	34075	34079	34090	34097	34110
35006	35009	35030	41306	82010	82017	82018						

59 locomotives on shed

Nos 30950/3/5/6/7 were Class 'Z' 0-8-0 tank locomotives introduced in 1929 and used for heavy shunting. Weighing 71 tons, they were allocated to this depot for the purpose of assisting trains up the steep gradient between Exeter St David's and Central stations.

Dawlish, by 'Grange' Class 4-6-0 locomotive No 6829 *Burmington Grange*.

Entry to our next depot, EXETER (83C) was once again unofficial, via the side of the platform! This was an 'all-steam' depot with 24 locomotives noted, of which four were Class '1400' 0-4-2 tanks, Nos 1420, 1451, 1462 and 1471. No 1420 still carried its former shedplate of 81C (Southall).

We then caught a Devon General double-decker bus to Exmouth Junction (my first visit). This was a very large single-ended depot consisting of 13 roads, one being a repair road. It was the largest Southern Region engine shed in the West Country and at various times had sub-sheds at no fewer than seven locations: Bude, Exmouth, Lyme Regis, Okehampton, Seaton, Callington

and Launceston.

We returned to the Central station by bus. Bulleid 'Pacific' No 34049 *Anti Aircraft Command* then hauled us to Salisbury where it came off. We were then steam-hauled on our final stage to Portsmouth by Class 'U' 2-6-0 locomotive No 31614. We arrived at Fratton station at 12.55 am (Monday). It had been an enjoyable summer day's excursion.

SOUTHERN REGION RAILROVER

SATURDAY 5 TO FRIDAY 11 SEPTEMBER

This was the first time I had purchased a Southern Region Railrover ticket - it cost £6

(Second Class). Local rail enthusiasts accompanying me for the week were Bill Jenkins and Jim 'Jimpy' Lawrence. I had sent to London for our tickets, collecting them from Fratton station on the first day of our adventure. A very rough timetable for the week ahead was planned, the SR

timetable was purchased and consulted, we briefly outlined our visits and decided on which days to travel.

Applications for permits to visit the majority of the installations were posted off two weeks prior to the Railrover. We had decided to start on Saturday and end on

The front cover and inside of the Railrover ticket.

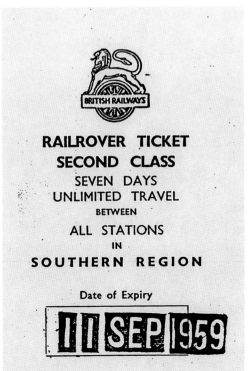

Friday, this giving us seven days. I had decided to take my father's 1926 Brownie box camera with me, but for some unknown reason very few pictures were taken - perhaps a film was lost or negatives were unprintable.

SATURDAY 5 SEPTEMBER (Day 1)

Our departure from Fratton was on the 7.56 am electric unit train to Brighton. On arrival we changed train and travelled to Hastings, where a further change was made. We next picked up a fast electric train to Ashford, Kent. 'Hastings' diesel units Nos 1017, 1019 and 1031 were noted near Hastings.

We walked from Ashford station to the locomotive depot.

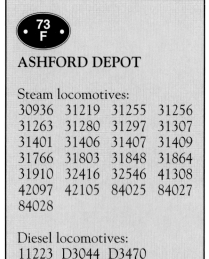

73 F

ASHFORD DEPOT

Steam locomotives:
30936 31219 31255 31256
31263 31280 31297 31307
31401 31406 31407 31409
31766 31803 31848 31864
31910 32416 32546 41308
42097 42105 84025 84027
84028

Diesel locomotives:
11223 D3044 D3470

28 locomotives on shed

We then caught the 2.30 pm train from Ashford to Dover, being steam-hauled by 'West Country' 4-6-2 locomotive No 34003 *Plymouth*. Departure from Dover (Priory) station was late afternoon; we travelled to Ramsgate, where we changed trains, catching a stopping train to Gillingham, Kent, via Faversham. We then made the early evening 5-minute

Note: When travelling on Railrovers the number of locomotives noted between stations and depot visits was often numerous, so to minimise space I have listed locomotives noted 'on line' at the end of each day, under a single heading.

DAY 1: NOTED ON LINE

Steam locomotives:
 4616   4626 30049 30132
30451 30711 30771 30850
30855 30900 30912 30914
30917 30922 30928 30929
30933 30934 30935 31037
31107 31128 31218 31252
31269 31272 31326 31337
31405 31481 31487 31530
31556 31614 31638 31695
31721 31741 31749 31775
31777 31804 31810 31820
31854 31855 31862 31866
31869 31898 31901 31909
32339 32340 32342 32343
32345 32350 32449 32475
32480 32504 32512 32519
32532 32553 33002 33032
33034 34001 34006 34021
34027 34037 34063 34064
34067 34068 34082 34084
34085 34088 34098 34100
34103 41290 41309 41310
42075 42076 42078 42095
42103 73083 73084 73088
80019 80145 80150 80152
80154 84020 84022 84023
84024 84026

Diesels locomotives:
11001 D3046 D3101 D3217
D3219 D3465 D3467 D3670
D3720 D3721 D5001 D5002
D5007 D5011 15228

Electric locomotives:
E5001 E5005 E5006 E5009
20003

walk to the engine shed, a small three-road depot.

73 D

GILLINGHAM DEPOT

Steam locomotives:
31244 31268 31481 31519
31575 31682 31719 33037

8 locomotives on shed

On leaving the depot we caught a train to London (Victoria). En route we noted 'Battle of Britain' Class 4-6-2 locomotive No 34085 *501 Squadron* employed on the 'Golden Arrow'. We then made our way back to Portsmouth travelling via Waterloo, Guildford and Havant to Fratton.

Estimated number of miles travelled on the first day: 285.

SUNDAY 6 SEPTEMBER (Day 2)

The day began by catching the 8.06 am train from Fratton to Eastleigh, via Botley. We were steam-hauled by Standard Class '5' 4-6-0 locomotive No 73115.

Steam locomotives of note in Eastleigh Works yard were No 82, the preserved Class 'A1X' 0-6-0 tank built in 1880. It was works shunter at Brighton for many years, having been withdrawn in 1946. Restored to its original livery at Clapham Museum, it was on show at Waterloo in 1948 in that station's centenary celebrations.

Also of note in the yard was No 563, the preserved Class 'T3' 4-4-0 locomotive. An express type introduced in 1893, it had exceptionally large driving wheels of 7 ft 1 in diameter. Condemned in 1939, due to the outbreak of war it was reinstated and ran again until 1945. It then lay derelict for three years at Eastleigh works yard before being restored to its original condition.

In the accompanying depot list

EASTLEIGH DEPOT

Steam locomotives:

5380	7308	30028	30030	30032	30048	30053	30056	30083	30109	30110	30117	30120
30125	30200	30212	30229	30287	30288	30289	30300	30306	30316	30328	30357	30377
30452	30456	30457	30474	30479	30480	30491	30498	30502	30503	30511	30514	30515
30531	30537	30668	30702	30732	30769	30770	30771	30773	30780	30784	30785	30786
30788	30790	30791	30802	30803	30805	30834	30843	30851	30853	30854	30856	30857
30858	30862	31618	31632	31735	31795	31801	32491	32510	32556	32559	32579	32694
33020	33021	33023	34024	35003	41293	41305	42089	73112	76011	76012	76013	76014
76015	76018	76025	76026	76061	76064	76068	82013	82014	82015			

Diesel locomotive:
13012

102 locomotives on shed

Class 'D1' 4-4-0 No 31735 was under repair in the depot works, an exile from Kent due to dieselisation in that area and a regular visitor to Fratton. Fratton-allocated Class 'E1' 0-6-0 tank No 32694 (which was used extensively on the dockyard goods) was on shed, on its way to the works for overhaul.

Leaving Eastleigh we travelled to Salisbury via Chandlers Ford and Romsey. We were then steam-

EXETER DEPOT

Steam locomotives:

1420	1440	1452	1468
1471	3606	3794	3804
4905	4917	4948	4999
5412	5524	6003	6385
6402	6406	6414	6842
6868	6965	7019	7253
7311	7316	7716	9497
9629	9765		

Diesel locomotive:
D3521

31 locomotives on shed

EXMOUTH JUNCTION DEPOT

Steam locomotives:

30023	30027	30044	30045
30182	30232	30317	30323
30327	30338	30374	30449
30450	30583	30584	30667
30669	30670	30676	30691
30718	30719	30825	30828
30844	30846	30950	30952
30953	30954	31831	31832
31835	31839	31841	31843
31844	31845	31849	32697
34009	34023	34034	34035
34051	34056	34062	34076
34104	34106	34109	35013
35016	35019	35020	82011
82024			

57 locomotives on shed

hauled to Exeter Central by 'Merchant Navy' 4-6-2 locomotive No 35020 *Bibby Line*. We then caught a local train from Central to St David's station.

We next caught a local train from the Central station to Poesloe Bridge Halt, the first stop

on the Exmouth branch line. This halt took us near our next shed, Exmouth Junction.

We returned to Exeter Central station where we departed at 3.20 pm, being steam-hauled to Yeovil Junction by 'Battle of Britain' 4-6-2 locomotive No 34109 *Sir Trafford Leigh-Mallory*. On arrival we transferred to the waiting Yeovil Town branch train, and were then steam-hauled to the Town station by Class 'M7' 0-4-4 tank locomotive No 30131. Entry to the engine shed, a small, compact three-road depot, was via the end of the station platform.

On our return to the Junction station we were once again hauled

YEOVIL DEPOT

Steam locomotives:

3671	3733	4636	4656
5548	5563	8745	9732
9764	30129	30796	30823
30841	31610	31613	31623
31790	34081	34110	76006

20 locomotives on shed

by No 30131, a push-and-pull-fitted tank. We then caught the 4.12 pm from Yeovil Junction to Templecombe, being steam-hauled by Class 'U' 2-6-0 locomotive No 31790. It was then just a 5-minute walk to the engine shed, a narrow, two-road brick-built shed.

TEMPLECOMBE DEPOT

Steam locomotives:
3765	40537	40563	40564
40634	40652	41248	43216
43218	43436	43682	43914
44102	44424	44557	47542
53805	53806	53808	73052
82039			

21 locomotives on shed

This was our final depot on this second day of the Railrover. We returned home to Fratton travelling via Salisbury, Romsey, Southampton Central and Fareham.

Estimated number of miles travelled on the second day: 260.

DAY 2: NOTED ON LINE

Steam locomotives:
82	563	4136	6827
7003	30021	30128	30131
30582	30674	30767	30778
30804	30951	30955	30957
31836	31852	32495	34015
34030	34033	34050	34053
34059	34079	34080	34081
34097	34098	35011	41306
41318	73085	76005	82013
82017	82018	82019	82022

Diesel locomotives:
DS1169 D3522

Petrol locomotive:
DS49

MONDAY 7 SEPTEMBER
(Day 3)

I met Bill and Jim at Fratton station and we departed on the 8.58 am electric unit train to Brighton, where on arrival we changed trains to the 10.25 am electric unit train to London (Victoria). We had planned to have a 'flit round' the suburbs of South London before eventually reaching Tonbridge depot. Our roundabout route took us from Victoria to Wimbledon via Clapham Junction, West Croydon and Mitcham Junction - at Wimbledon we changed trains and travelled to Guildford via Effingham Junction. Another change was made at Guildford; we were steam-hauled by Standard Class '4' 2-6-0 locomotive No 76056 to Redhill and then diesel-hauled by No D5014 between Redhill and Tonbridge via Nutfield, Godstone, Edenbridge, Penshurst and Leigh.

Of note on passing Redhill depot (75B) were two steam locomotives stored at the rear of the shed, Nos 31247, a Class 'D1' 4-4-0, and 31771, a Class 'L' 4-4-0. Both had tarpaulins covering their chimneys.

TONBRIDGE DEPOT

Steam locomotives:
31164	31177	31193	31278
31319	31322	31327	31481
31489	31521	31590	31825
31875	31879	31901	31906
31907	32580	33024	33028
33030	33033	33036	33040
80012	80145		

Diesel locomotive:
D2276

27 locomotives on shed

On our arrival at Tonbridge we made the 5-minute walk to the depot, a six-road straight shed with a turntable.

Our next depot of the visit was Tunbridge Wells West. We were steam-hauled to this station by Standard Class '4' 2-6-4 tank locomotive No 80014, our route being via High Brooms and Tunbridge Wells Central. On arrival we entered the shed via a gate in the station yard. This four-road straight shed was set in pleasant rural surroundings with the station visible from the shed yard.

TUNBRIDGE WELLS WEST DEPOT

Steam locomotives:
30533	31266	31310	32581
42066	42069	42087	42103
42106	80014	80016	80153

12 locomotives on shed

On the way back to London we travelled on a 'Hastings' diesel unit train - our destination was Waterloo East (high level), via Lewisham. 'Hastings' units noted on this journey were Nos 1001, 1002, 1003, 1012, 1013, 1014, 1016, 1017, 1033 and 1035.

It was mid-evening when we arrived at Waterloo. We visited some other main-line stations and then got the 8.50 pm train from Waterloo to Portsmouth.

Estimated number of miles travelled on the third day: 300.

EUSTON

Steam locomotives:
45288	45324	46157	46168
47304	47529	47669	80038

ST PANCRAS

Steam locomotives:
45273 45342 45616

KING'S CROSS

Steam locomotives:
60013 60076 60148 60158
60885 67776 69581 69593

Diesel locomotives:
'Deltic' D201 D5301 D5311
D5313 D5318 D5904 D5905
D5909

'Deltic' was a numberless prototype diesel-electric locomotive, with distinctive bright blue livery and displaying the word DELTIC on its sides. Introduced in 1955 and built at Derby Works, 'Deltic' worked trials on the Midland Region during 1957 and 1958. It was the forerunner of the D9000 series on the King's Cross to Edinburgh expresses, later being used on only King's Cross to North of England expresses. It was never taken into British Railways stock and remained the property of the builder. Weight: 106 tons. Now preserved in the Science Museum, South Kensington, London. This was the first time that I had noted 'Deltic'.

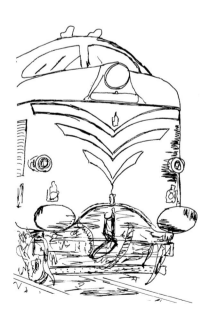

The impressive 'American style' front of 'Deltic', noted at King's Cross.

DAY 3: NOTED ON LINE

Steam locomotives:

4672	30249	30321	30517
30520	30770	30863	30902
30905	30914	30930	31247
31308	31317	31487	31512
31517	31533	31617	31628
31634	31635	31693	31724
31756	31771	31793	31798
31799	31803	31822	31862
31863	31867	31872	31877
31878	31892	31896	31899
31909	31917	31923	32165
32340	32444	32447	32450
32521	32539	32544	32545
33004	33006	33015	33017
33026	33032	33034	33039
34001	34003	34026	34052
34063	34073	34078	34084
42066	42082	42091	42105
73086	75075	76054	80152

Diesel locomotives:

11221	11226	D3049	D3094
D3224	D3461	D3464	D3465
D3469	D3669	15201	15212
15214	15225	15232	

Electric locomotive:
20002

TUESDAY 8 SEPTEMBER (Day 4)

The day started at Portsmouth & Southsea (Low Level), catching the 8.30 am train to Southampton Central; we were steam-hauled by Standard Class '4' 2-6-0 locomotive No 76069 (71A). At Southampton we crossed the footbridge and boarded the Salisbury train, being steam-hauled by 'Merchant Navy' 4-6-2 locomotive No 35030 *Elder Dempster Lines*. Our route was via Nursling, Romsey, Dunbridge and Dean.

On passing Southampton Docks we noted Class 'E1' 0-6-0 tank No 32689. Introduced in 1874, this tank was still in active use.

A change of locomotive was made at Salisbury, and we then travelled via Templecombe and Yeovil to Exeter. Our departure from St David's station for our destination of Barnstaple Junction depot was at about 1 pm. The steam locomotive which hauled us was 'Battle of Britain' 4-6-2 No 34079 *141 Squadron*. On our arrival at the small North Devon town of Barnstaple we were greeted by bright sunshine, so we decided to take a walk around the town. We purchased food and drink and some small souvenirs, including a stick of Devon rock to take home with us.

Returning to the station we checked our departure time, then visited the engine shed. This small, two-road straight shed was

BARNSTAPLE JUNCTION DEPOT

Steam locomotives:

6343	30033	30247	30251
30254	30255	30375	30691
31832	31838	34030	41294
41295	41314		

14 locomotives on shed

DAY 4: NOTED ON LINE

Steam locomotives:

2831	3808	4176	6333
6870	30021	30044	30071
30131	30507	30524	30532
30582	30669	30715	30798
30832	30846	30858	30909
30912	30954	30957	31633
31795	31837	32689	33020
34033	34056	34065	34076
34096	35001	35002	35007
35010	35026	40563	43436
47542	73050	75072	75073
76005	76060	82011	82025

situated almost next to the station - we gained entrance via the station yard. This was the only depot visited on this day.

Departure for Exeter was at 3.45 pm - we took the same route home as on the forward journey.

Estimated number of miles travelled on the fourth day: 300.

WEDNESDAY 9 SEPTEMBER (Day 5)

We caught the 7.22 am train from Fratton to London (Victoria), then transferred to another electric unit train and travelled to London Bridge where we picked up a train to Gravesend, our route being via Belvedere and Dartford. On our arrival at Gravesend station we walked through the town to the River Thames. We then purchased single tickets to Tilbury; the fare was 7d. This journey, as were all those by tube train, was additional to our Railrover ticket.

We passed Tilbury terminus station on our way to the engine shed, a corrugated iron four-road straight-through shed. It was, at

Below Class '4' 2-6-4T No 42220 on shed at Tilbury (33B).

Below right The water tower at Ramsgate depot.

this visit, very run down.

Following this visit we returned to Gravesend via the ferry, then caught an electric train to Ramsgate, travelling via Chatham, Strood and Faversham. We walked to the depot, which was a six-road block-end straight shed, situated in close proximity to a carriage cleaning shed. Its code was 73G, formerly 74B; this re-coding from a 'B' to a 'G' was reflected in the

TILBURY DEPOT

Steam locomotives:
42220 42524 42527 47328
80072 80080 80103 80105

8 locomotives on shed

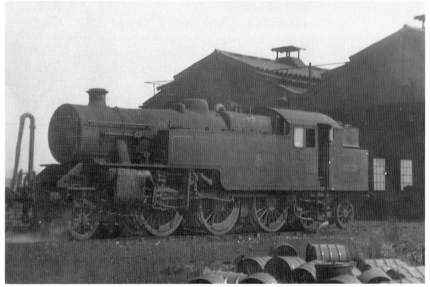

RAMSGATE DEPOT

Steam locomotives:
30930 31324 31500 31501
31592 31743 31749 34003
42076 84026

10 locomotives on shed

Diesel meets steam: Nos D5006 and 31820 at Dover Depot.

Left Withdrawn Class 'D' 4-4-0 locomotive No 31501 rusts away its last
years in Ramsgate depot yard.
Introduced in 1901, this class was
designed by Wainwright for the SE&CR.
Its 6 ft 8 in driving wheels and six-wheel
tender made it an ideal secondary passenger locomotive. Prior to 1950 No 31501
was allocated to Faversham depot code
(73E), then later to Ashford, from
which it found its way to Ramsgate in
the mid-1950s. As can be seen, the boiler casing has been removed and no doubt
many other fittings and fixtures from the
cab. It stood here until mid or late 1962
before it was scrapped. *For this information
I am indebted to J. H. Websper (Margate)
and R. Yates (Ramsgate)*

generally run-down state that the
building and the yard was in at the
date of this visit. Both the coaling
and water facilities were prominent features.

We then returned to the station
where we caught the 3.40 pm train
to Dover. We were hauled by
'West Country' Class 4-6-2 No
34026 *Yes Tor*.

It was early evening as we made
the 20-minute walk via Market
Square to the engine shed, which
was situated near Dover Marine
station adjacent to the sea wall.
This five-road straight shed,
together with a repair road, was
quite active, but the structure was
in a very run-down condition. Its
former code was 74C.

It is worth noting that no fewer
than 12 Bulleid 'Pacifics' were
seen at Dover, 11 being 'Battle of
Britain' and one 'West Country'.

We then made the return walk

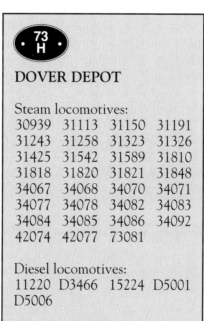

DOVER DEPOT

Steam locomotives:
30939 31113 31150 31191
31243 31258 31323 31326
31425 31542 31589 31810
31818 31820 31821 31848
34067 34068 34070 34071
34077 34078 34082 34083
34084 34085 34086 34092
42074 42077 73081

Diesel locomotives:
11220 D3466 15224 D5001
D5006

Electric locomotive:
E5001

37 locomotives on shed

to Dover Priory station. It was
starting to get dark as we prepared
for our journey home to
Portsmouth; Bill Jenkins and Jim
Lawrence suggested we travel via
London rather than Canterbury,
Hastings and Brighton, but I
decided to take the Canterbury
route and Bill and Jim the London

route - it was a case of 'see who
gets home first'. It was decided
before we went our separate ways
that we would meet at Fratton
station the next morning at
10.25 am.

I was steam-hauled between
Dover Priory and Canterbury West
by Standard Class '2' 2-6-2 tank
locomotive No 84023. On my
arrival at Brighton station I asked
the ticket collector 'When is the
next train to Portsmouth?' He
glanced at his watch, which read
10.20 pm, and replied '6 am
tomorrow morning'. I had missed
the last train home!

I could have caught a train to
Victoria, then made my way to
Waterloo, probably connecting
with the last train or a morning
papers train to Portsmouth, but I
decided against this. Instead I
caught a train to West Worthing
where I alighted and waited about
15 minutes for the Bognor train.
The ticket collector at West
Worthing said 'You'll probably get
a connection at Bognor'.

I arrived at Bognor at about
11 pm and asked if the Portsmouth
train had left; the ticket collector
said 'Yes.' I could have hitched a
lift home, but as I had never had
any hitching experience before I

decided against this method.

It was a very cool, mild night with no wind, so I was lucky with the weather. I took a walk round Bognor shops, purchasing a bag of chips and a cold drink which I consumed as I walked about the town. Returning to the railway station about midnight, I hoped to get some sleep in the waiting room, but much to my dismay I found that the station entrance had been locked up.

I therefore returned to the town and then to the sea front hoping to find a cosy shelter to sleep in - but the presence of several tramps in this area made me go elsewhere. Returning once again to the station vicinity I passed a large garage with about half a dozen cars parked in its forecourt. I was very tired by now, so I decided to try and make a bed on one of the car's running-boards hidden from the view of any passers-by. This I did - not very comfortable, but good enough for me to get several hours' sleep! I kept waking up during the night to replace my haversack which I was using as a pillow and which kept falling on the ground.

I was awake again at 5.30 am. I had a quick drink of lemonade left over from the previous night, said 'goodbye' to the Austin 7 which had been my bed and then started walking to the station. I caught the aroma of fresh bread being baked as I made my way, so I purchased a small loaf. This would be my early breakfast on the train to Portsmouth.

The sun was just rising and it promised to be another fine, sunny day. I had to wait until the station opened at 5.45 am before I could show a somewhat surprised ticket collector my railway ticket. He mentioned something about making an early start, but I didn't carry on the conversation! I boarded an electric train, and after changing at Barnham I fell asleep - but instinct must have told me that I

had arrived home. As the train jerked to a halt I looked out of the window to see the station sign 'Fratton'. The station clock showed 6.30 am.

I had obviously made the wrong decision at Dover the previous night!

Estimated number of miles travelled on the fifth day: 310.

DAY 5: NOTED ON LINE

Steam locomotives:

30248	30513	30915	30922
30929	30932	31162	31326
31404	31530	31583	31725
31819	31855	31878	32105
32450	32522	32551	32661
33002	33037	34073	41312
42105	42509	42520	84022
90256			

Diesel locomotives:

11130	D3098	D3220	13225
D3459	D5003	D5009	D5014
15229			

Electric:

E5002   E5006

THURSDAY 10 SEPTEMBER (Day 6)

Having recovered sufficiently from the previous night out, I was woken by the sound of the alarm clock at 9 am. I had a quick breakfast then gathered some food and drink for the day ahead. My arrival at the entrance to Fratton station was eagerly awaited by Bill Jenkins and Jim Lawrence who told me that they had both arrived home safely the previous night from Dover. I then told them my story and they both had a good laugh!

We travelled on the 10.32 am stopping train to Waterloo, changing at Weybridge, from where we caught a train to Feltham, travelling via Staines Central. On our arrival we made the very long walk

---

70 B

FELTHAM DEPOT

Steam locomotives:

30031	30177	30179	30339
30453	30494	30495	30497
30502	30503	30504	30517
30518	30519	30520	30567
30687	30689	30777	30834
30839	31033	31246	31494
31509	31545	31727	31892
33013	33016	33027	33038

Diesel locomotives:

D3040   D3041   D3042

35 locomotives on shed

---

to Feltham depot. The weather was extremely hot - in fact, we noted a thermometer in a shop window which showed 83 degrees. On our return to Feltham station we caught a train to Waterloo, travelling via Twickenham and Clapham Junction. We then crossed the road to the high-level platforms, A, B, C and D, and picked up a Charing Cross to Dover express from platform 'C'. We were steam-hauled by 'West Country' 4-6-2 locomotive No 34012 *Launceston* to Ashford; for some reason we visited Ashford depot twice on this Railrover.

ASHFORD DEPOT (73G, formerly 74A) - there were 28 on shed which included four diesel shunters. The only named express engines noted here were two 'Schools' Class 4-4-0s, Nos 30936 *Cranleigh* and 30937 *Epsom*.

Returning to the station by bus, we then caught a train to Waterloo, travelling via Maidstone East, Otford and Swanley. From the high-level at Waterloo we then travelled via Lewisham to Hither Green to visit the depot.

No DS1173, an 0-6-0 diesel shunter allocated to the Engineer's Dept, at Hither Green

73 C

HITHER GREEN DEPOT

Steam locomotives:
31253	31268	31414	31688
31690	31694	31725	31756
31857	31858	31859	31880
31922	31923	31925	33031
48360	68917	68991	

Diesel locomotives:
DS1173	11226	D3097	D3099
D5001	D5003	D5006	D5010
D5013	15202	15219	15222

31 locomotives on shed

Of note, as on previous visits to this shed, were both LMS and ER steam locomotives (Nos 48360, 68917 and 68991 in the above list) - these had been employed on transfer freight trains from North London.

We returned to Portsmouth via Waterloo, Guildford and Havant.

Estimated number of miles travelled on the sixth day: 280.

DAY 6: NOTED ON LINE

Steam locomotives:
4634	7324	30089	30133
30245	30321	30378	30450
30506	30540	30701	30786
30824	30835	30931	31164
31177	31219	31223	31253
31259	31278	31322	31327
31401	31407	31480	31489
31519	31588	31615	31630
31688	31722	31753	31868
31869	31876	31877	31878
31880	32438	32500	33006
33007	33012	33017	33026
33031	33032	33039	34006
34028	34062	34089	34103
35002	35008	35012	35021
41309	42092	84020	

Diesel locomotives:
D3048 D3092 D3471

WEDNESDAY 11 SEPTEMBER (Day 7)

After six days in the company of Bill and Jim, I decided for the final day of the ticket to travel with my mother and father and let my two companions visit depots on their own. Our route for the day was via Waterloo to Liverpool Street and then to Stratford where the open-air market was visited. We returned to the city to visit some shopping areas and get a meal. Our return to Portsmouth was on the 7.50 pm train from Waterloo.

Estimated number of miles travelled on the seventh day: 170.

Estimated number of miles travelled during the week: 1,905.

DAY 7: NOTED ON LINE

Steam locomotives:
30929	34078	43149	44294
61372	61607	61886	61908
64670	64694	67732	68613
68665	70003	70009	70013
70038	70039		

Diesel:
D0226	D3631	D3633	D5518
D5522	D5536		

No D0226 was a 0-6-0 shunter introduced in 1957 and used for comparison trials between electric and hydraulic transmission. It carried a black livery and was noted hauling a passenger train near Stratford.

SOUTHAMPTON

SATURDAY 7 NOVEMBER

I went on this visit to the docks with local railway enthusiast Mike Yerbury. Our departure was on the 9.06 am train from Fratton, and the return fare was 5/4d.

We walked to the docks via the Bargate. I had previously sent for and received a fishing permit to enter the Old Docks. However, some difficulty was experienced in locating the engine shed, but it was eventually found. It was quite

BETWEEN FRATTON AND SOUTHAMPTON

Steam locomotives:
30349   30788   31620   31638
31795   31797   32694   34010
76009

Diesel locomotive:
15214

a small building consisting of three roads - we could easily have passed it by. It is of note that a sub-depot, known as the New Docks, existed about half a mile west of this depot.

We walked around the docks noting steam engines shunting and awaiting their duties. Some were employed on Boat Trains to and from London (Waterloo).

Eleven out of the 17 locomotives noted in the Docks were Class 'USA' 0-6-0 tanks. These American-style steam locomotives were all allocated to Southampton

Right The letter I received (dated 11 August 1956) permitting entry to Southampton Old Docks.

Below The front and reverse of the permit used. I had originally intended to visit this depot in August 1956, but it never materialised. This permit was kept and then used on this visit.

BRITISH TRANSPORT COMMISSION   (2486A/71)
~~DOCKS & INLAND WATERWAYS EXECUTIVE~~

——————— TIW

R. P. BIDDLE, C.B.E.
Docks & Marine Manager
W. F. GRIFFITHS
Asst. Docks Manager
Telegrams FOREMOST, SOUTHAMPTON
Telephone SOUTHAMPTON 23838
Extension   365
IN YOUR REPLY PLEASE
QUOTE THIS REFERENCE

ED. 571

DOCKS & MARINE MANAGER'S OFFICE
DOCK HOUSE
SOUTHAMPTON

11th August, 1956.

Dear Sir,

    With reference to your letter of the 10th August, Southampton Docks generally are not open to visitors but as a special case I am prepared to arrange for you to enter the Old Docks in order to visit the Locomotive Depot on any one day during the period you mention.

    I enclose herewith the necessary Permit together with an Indemnity Form and shall be glad if you will arrange for the latter to be completed and returned to me as soon as possible.

    Will you please note that in the case of applicants under twenty-one years of age the Indemnity Form must be signed by a parent or guardian on their behalf, as well as by an independent witness.

    I must draw your attention to the fact that permission to visit the Motive Power Depot is granted subject to the condition that British Railways will not be responsible for the death or injury of any person exercising this permission whilst on the Commission's premises, nor for any loss or damage to the property of any such person however such death, injury, loss or damage may be caused, and whether or not by the act, neglect or default of the Commission, their servants or agents.

    Yours faithfully,

R. P. Biddle

Mr. M.G. Harvey,
75 Penhale Road,
Fratton,
PORTSMOUTH,
Hants.

Encl:

BRITISH TRANSPORT COMMISSION   (5333)
THE DOCKS & INLAND WATERWAYS
(referred to in this Permit as "the Commission")
(SOUTHAMPTON DOCKS)

PERMIT
to go upon Dock Premises subject to the following
CONDITIONS

The holder is permitted in accordance with the terms of the application and instruction signed by him/her or on his/her behalf to go upon the Dock premises at SOUTHAMPTON DOCKS on the   **SEE OVER**   day of 19   subject to the Bye-laws applicable to the said premises and to the regulations and conditions relating to passengers and their property (in so far as they are applicable to the said premises and are not inconsistent herewith) and to the further condition that the holder will be responsible for and will release and indemnify the Commission and any other bodies or persons owning, working, occupying or using the said premises (whether jointly with the Commission or otherwise) and their servants and agents from and against all liability for, personal injury (whether fatal or otherwise), loss of or damage to property and any other loss, damage, delay, detention, costs and expenses however caused or incurred (whether or not by the act or neglect of the Commission or of any such other bodies or persons or of their servants or agents respectively) which but for the exercise by the holder of such permission would have not arisen.

This Permit is the property of the Commission and must be produced and delivered up upon demand by any officer or servant of the Commission and returned to the Docks and Marine Manager or his duly authorised representative upon expiration or cancellation.

DATED this   **11th**   day of   August,   19 **56**
R. P. BIDDLE,
Docks and Marine Manager

Issued by......................

MR. M.G. HARVEY.

LOCOMOTIVE DEPOT, OLD DOCKS.

AVAILABLE ANY ONE DAY FROM
AUGUST 13TH – 18TH, 1956.
(INCLUSIVE)

SOUTHAMPTON DOCKS DEPOT

Steam locomotives:
30069   32109   32151

3 locomotives on shed

SOUTHAMPTON DOCKS

Steam locomotives:
30061   30063   30064   30065
30066   30067   30068   30071
30073   30074   30788   31631
32108   32689

Diesel locomotive:
11222

Docks depot (71I) and carried the number series 30061-74 (14 in all). They were introduced in 1942 to a US Transportation Corps design, and were purchased by the Southern Railway in 1946. They were fitted with modified cabs and coal bunkers and some other detail differences for use in Southampton Docks.

Also of interest on shed was

Class 'E2' 0-6-0 tank No 32109 of 1915 vintage and Class 'E1' 0-6-0 tank No 32151, introduced in 1874 - 85 years old and still in working order!

Whilst in Southampton Docks we visited the carriage shed, which was situated in the New Docks. We noted the following named steam Pullman carriages: 'Aurora', 'Clementina', 'Florence',

'Hawthorn', 'Juno', 'Niobe', 'Ruby' and 'Topaz'.

We had completed our visit to the Docks at 1 pm, and returning to the city centre we purchased a dinner at Woolworths. After a short rest we walked to The Dell, the home ground of Southampton Football Club, where we watched the match against Queens Park Rangers, the home side winning 2-1. After the game we made the long walk to the Terminus station where we noted Standard Class '4' 2-6-0 No 76069. Our final walk was to the Central station where we caught a 'Hampshire' diesel unit train home to Fratton. We must have walked about six miles in all, but it had been an interesting first visit to Southampton Docks shed (71I) and area.

Arrival at Fratton station was at 7.30 pm.

ADDITIONAL HIGHLIGHTS OF 1959

EASTLEIGH DEPOT (71A): SUNDAY 22 MARCH - 113 steam and 11 diesel shunters were on shed. Of note was Exmouth Junction-allocated Class 'E1/R' 0-6-2 tank engine No 32135; also of note was once again the Class 'C14' 0-4-0 tank No 77S (71A) used at Redbridge Sleeper Works. Two aging tanks, Class 'B4' 0-4-0s Nos 30088 and 30096, were also on shed, and I took a photograph of the latter, accompanied by a 'Q1' Class 0-6-0.

WOLVERHAMPTON: SUNDAY 29 MARCH - On this Easter Sunday excursion from Portsmouth (fare 22/9d) we visited Oxley (84B), Stafford Road (84A) and Bushbury (3B), all second visits for me. We also visited Wolverhampton (Stafford Road) Works, my first visit. We did not attempt to enter via the main gate but gained entry via the rear gate in Gorsebrooke Road. However, we could not gain admittance to

the works, so the locomotives in this list were noted through the windows of the building.

READING, OXFORD AND SWINDON: MONDAY 24 MAY - This was a trip arranged by Portsmouth schoolteacher Jack Stillwell. The party of 13 travelled at a cost of 15 shillings each.

First visited was Reading (81D) where we noted 58 steam and four diesels. We then moved on to

WOLVERHAMPTON (STAFFORD ROAD) WORKS

Steam locomotives:
2851   5912   6011   6126
6314   6367   6415

7 locomotives in Works

Class 'B4' 0-4-0 tank No 30096 dwarfed by Class 'Q1' 0-6-0 No 33021.

Standard Class '4' 4-6-0 locomotive No 75008 at Oxford depot (81F). *J. Stillwell*

'Modified Hall' 4-6-0 No 7906 *Fron Hall* at Oxford. *J. Stillwell*

Oxford (81F) where we noted 47 steam which included Eastern Region Class 'K3/2' 2-6-0 No 61817.

We were steam-hauled between Oxford and Swindon Junction by Eastern Region Class 'B1' 4-6-0 locomotive No 61201 of Leicester depot (15E).

Under construction at Swindon Works were Class '9F' 2-10-0 steam locomotives Nos 92207 to 92212, and diesel locomotives Nos D806 to D818 and D2114 to D2118. Also sighted was Bromsgrove-allocated 'banker' Class '9F' No 92079, unique in that it was fitted with a headlamp. As a sign of the increasing number of steam engines being scrapped, the accompanying list of locomotives were noted in the scrapyard.

SWINDON SCRAPYARD			
Steam locomotives:			
1401	1423	1429	1437
1456	1457	1467	2254
2803	2812	2823	2825
2830	2833	4200	4226
4261	4377	4540	4553
4584	5315	5355	5382
5386	5388	5390	5400
5404	5509	5566	5703
5708	5733	5743	5810
6318	6322	6328	6331
6354	6409	6428	6721
6723	6727	7738	

47 locomotives noted

The 'Happy Bunch' lined up in front of Collett-designed 'Manor' 4-6-0 No 7801 *Anthony Manor* in Swindon Works yard. The photograph was taken by one of the young school-boys in our party of 13. Those pictured, left to right, are: Jim Lawrence (running - didn't quite make it for the line-up!), four school-boys, Michael Harvey, Eddie Rooke, Jack Stillwell, David Bodenham, 'Jes' Lilly and another school-boy. On the extreme right, with hand raised, is Charlie Best.

LONDON: SATURDAY 4 JULY - Once again, as on previous London visits, we made an early start, catching the 5.32 am 'workman's train' from Fratton to Waterloo (fare 13/8d). I travelled in four-carriage suburban unit No 4338 with David Copus and 'Stan', who lived at this date in Hyde Park Road, Southsea. Some brief notes on depots visited:

HITHER GREEN (73C) - Eleven 'C' Class 0-6-0s, seven ER engines and seven diesels. 32 on shed.

OLD OAK COMMON (81A) - 69 steam and two diesels. 'Castle' Class 4-6-0 No 5014 *Goodrich Castle* displayed a 'Cornish Riviera' headboard. Five engines noted in the large depot works: Nos 4989, 5084, 6142, 9751 and 73023 (No 73023 carried a 6E Chester shedplate).

NEASDEN (14D) - 31 locomotives, all steam.

CRICKLEWOOD (14A) - 55 steam and four diesels.

CAMDEN (1B) - 55 locomotives, all steam.

KENTISH TOWN (14B) - 54 locomotives, all steam.

David Copus and 'Stan' visited Hornsey (34B) whilst I visited BRICKLAYERS ARMS (73B): 47 steam and one diesel shunter. My two companions paid 10d each for an Ordinary Child Return ticket from King's Cross to Hornsey.

BRIGHTON AND EASTBOURNE: WEDNESDAY 8 JULY - Travelling with David Bodenham, I visited Brighton depot (75A) where 35 steam and one diesel shunter were noted. Moving on to Eastbourne via Lewes, we passed the former depot. A visit was made to this depot which in the early 1950s had a code of 75G and later became a sub-shed of Brighton.

Of the seven steam engines at Eastbourne depot, at least three were in store. This closed and almost demolished seven-road shed was, at this date, in a very

EASTBOURNE DEPOT

Steam locomotives:
32339   32441   32494   32519
42090   42106   73041

7 locomotives on shed

run-down state; many tracks had been removed.

Steam locomotives noted 'on line' on this trip were: Nos 30050, 30052, 30544, 30545, 31492, 31896, 31899, 32341, 32344, 32479, 32509, 32646, 34019, 34098 and 80147.

HORSHAM AND THREE BRIDGES: FRIDAY 10 JULY -

As a follow-up trip to Brighton and Eastbourne we visited Horsham and Three Bridges.

Steam locomotives noted 'on line' on this trip were: Nos 30050, 30915, 31161, 31817, 31900, 32342, 32344, 76057 and 76069. Diesels: Nos 13270 and 15234. Electrics: Nos E5004, 20002 and 20003.

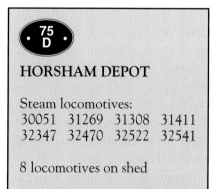

75 D

HORSHAM DEPOT

Steam locomotives:
30051   31269   31308   31411
32347   32470   32522   32541

8 locomotives on shed

75 E

THREE BRIDGES DEPOT

Steam locomotives:
30506   30547   31162   31327
31522   31530   31543   31813
32338   32350   32351   32450
32522   32527   32532   32534
32536   75070   80012

19 locomotives on shed

BRISTOL AND RADSTOCK: SUNDAY 16 AUGUST - This was a Cardiff excursion from Portsmouth Harbour. The travelling party included Mike Yerbury, Tony Ingram, 'Gasser', 'Cardiff' and Mike Worley, and the return fare was 12/6d. Steam haulage to Salisbury was by Class 'U' 2-6-0 locomotive No 31621, and from Salisbury to Bristol (Stapleton Road) by 'Castle' Class 4-6-0 No 7003 *Elmley Castle*. On arrival we were then steam-hauled to Temple Meads by Class '4500' 2-6-2 tank locomotive No 5554.

I was the only one in the party to hand in the forward half of my Portsmouth to Bristol excursion ticket to the ticket collector at Stapleton Road station, when I should have retained it, as the others did, until our arrival at Temple Meads station. Thus when the ticket collector at Temple Meads asked for my ticket, I only had the return half with me.

I explained to him what had happened, but he would not believe me, even though I showed him the return half, and the others in the party also handed in their forward tickets. He telephoned Stapleton Road station but could get no reply, so he finally let me through the barrier, but not before he had taken my name and address.

It had been agreed many trips previously that, if ever we had to give our name and address to a railway official, we would give the correct name but the address would be an 'odd' number in Priory Crescent, Milton, Portsmouth - this would be false as all the numbers in this road are even! On this particular occasion I had much pleasure in handing the 'awkward' ticket collector a non-existent address.

After all the fuss and time-wasting at the ticket barrier we eventually got away and made the walk to our first depot. Despite this setback we were all in a good mood and looking forward to our visits.

The first shed visited was BRISTOL (BATH ROAD) (82A) where we noted 46 steam locomotives on shed; a pannier tank from Yeovil (72C) was undergoing repairs in the depot works.

Our second depot was ST PHILIP'S MARSH (82B) where we noted 73 steam, seven diesel shunters and two WR diesel railcars.

The third depot of the visit was BARROW ROAD (82E) where we noted 42 steam and three diesel shunters. It was of note that Class '3F' 0-6-0 engine No 43520 still carried the words BRITISH RAILWAYS in full on its tender.

We then travelled by DMU to Bath Spa, and on arrival we walked to BATH (GREEN PARK) depot (82F). There were 30 steam locomotives on shed including six Class '7F' 2-8-0s and one Class '1P' 0-4-4 tank of 1895 vintage, No 58086.

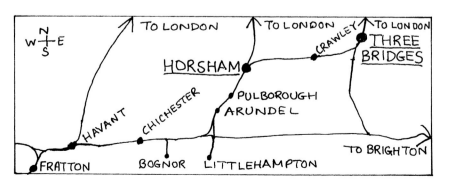

Left Six of these Class '7F' 2-8-0s, Nos 53801/2/3/5/7/10, were on shed at Bath (Green Park).

Below Two of these Sentinel geared engines were on shed at Radstock, Nos 47190 and 47191. These single-speed engines for the Somerset & Dorset Joint Railway were taken into LMS stock in 1930. All the other four tanks on shed were 'Jinty' 0-6-0s.

On leaving this depot I had a difference of opinion with my fellow companions - I decided to catch a bus to Radstock to visit the small two-road sub-depot of Bath (Green Park).

RADSTOCK DEPOT

Steam locomotives:
47190 47191 47275 47316
47465 47557

6 locomotives on shed

The remainder of the party decided to visit Westbury depot (82D). We agreed to meet up on the return excursion from Cardiff.

LONDON: SUNDAY 30 AUGUST - It had become almost a common feature to be transferred to a bus for part of a rail journey on a Sunday due to engineering work on the line; on this visit we had a bus between Guildford and Woking. Engine sheds visited were Willesden (1A), Camden (1B), Cricklewood (14A), Kentish Town (14B) and Neasden (14D), but the highlight of the day was our first ever visit to Nine Elms.

Nine Elms was a massive 25-road block-end straight shed, consisting of two sheds adjacent to each other, the old shed of 15 roads and the new one of 10 roads. All engines entered the shed via the turntable at the west end of the yard.

Many of the steam locomotives

⬭ 70 A   NINE ELMS DEPOT

Steam locomotives:
4698	9770	30133	30241	30248	30320	30321	30457	30489	30689	30694	30701	30774
30833	30851	30902	30903	30907	30909	30911	30912	30913	30919	31004	31112	31145
31227	31271	31495	31505	31507	31510	31552	31617	31624	31720	31754	31758	31760
31763	31768	31770	31785	31786	31787	31788	31789	31796	32487	32497	32498	32500
32563	33009	33015	33017	34009	34010	34016	34020	34029	34032	34034	34053	34075
34093	35018	35019	73085	73089	73115							

Diesel locomotives:
11221 D3049 D3226 15212 15213

76 locomotives on shed

BRITISH TRANSPORT COMMISSION.

MOTIVE POWER OFFICER,
SOUTHERN REGION, BRITISH RAILWAYS,
Reference   WATERLOO STATION.S.E.1.   27th April   19 59
My.HO.VS.

Dear Sir,   VISITS TO MOTIVE POWER DEPOTS.

     With reference to your letter of 24th April,1959.
     I regret it is not possible to issue the permit you desire as the
regulations on the Southern Region do NOT allow visits to Motive Power
Depots on the following days:-
****** 26th/31st MARCH,**15/19*MAY,and 31st JULY/4th AUGUST,1959.
     SATURDAYS during the period 1st/JUNE/30TH SEPTEMBER, 1959.
               VISITS CANNOT BE ARRANGED ON SUNDAYS
                         OR BANK HOLIDAYS
     Visits must be concluded by 5.0pm.
     If therefore you will select another day I shall be pleased to give
your application consideration.
***** Permits are not issued to persons under the age of 16, if you can
confirm that you have attained this age I shall be pleased to issue the
** necessary permit. ** Please give names and addresses of others in party,
** and show age of any under 16 years. ** On the other hand if you are not
yet 16 it will be necessary for you to be accompanied by an adult whose
name and address should be given.
     Owing to the large number of applications received daily it is
necessary for ten days' notice to be given of any proposed visit.
     It is regretted that no more than TWO Depots may be visited on any
one day.
     STEWARTS LANE,ASHFORD AND HITHER GRN. VISITS HAVE BEEN CANCELLED FOR
                              THE TIME BEING.

*** refers to your enquiry   Yours faithfully,
                                           for G.A.WEEDEN
Master D.G.Copus,   MOTIVE POWER OFFICER.
1, Fernhurst Road,
SOUTHSEA.

at Nine Elms were ex-South Eastern Section classes, being made redundant at this date due to the dieselisation and electrification in the Kent and East Sussex areas. The following list highlights these locomotives: Class 'C' 0-6-0s: 31004, 31112, 31227, 31271, 31495 and 31510; Class 'D1' 4-4-0s: 31145 and 31505; Class 'E1' 4-4-0: 31507; Class 'H' 0-4-4T: 31552; Class 'L1' 4-4-0s: 31754,31758, 31785, 31786, 31787, 31788 and 31789; Class 'L' 4-4-0s: 31760, 31763, 31768 and 31770.

STRATFORD (30A) was visited for the second time on 15 November - 173 steam and 68 diesels were on shed. The Works were also visited, where nine steam locomotives were undergoing repairs. The guide took us into the inspection pit beneath Class 'B1' 4-6-0 No 61043.

Above We had planned our Nine Elms trip well in advance. As stated in this letter, dated 27 April 1959, 'visits cannot be arranged on Sunday', but we applied and received permits dated Monday 31 August which we used on Sunday 30 August!

Right The permit used on the visit.

Nos 30902 to 30919 in the Nine Elms list were Class 'V' or 'Schools', the most powerful 4-4-0 in Europe.

BR 19141/1

BRITISH TRANSPORT COMMISSION
BRITISH RAILWAYS

Your Reference
Our Reference   MOTIVE POWER   17th August   1959
HO. VS   SOUTH

Dear Sir,

     In accordance with your request, I have been pleased to arrange for your visit(s)
to Motive Power Depot(s) as shewn below, and I hope you have an instructive and
enjoyable visit.

     On arrival at the Depot, this letter should be presented immediately at the
Depot office and a responsible member of the staff will conduct you round.

     In the interests of safety, no person under 16 years of age will be allowed to
visit a Motive Power Depot unless accompanied by an adult, and the visit must finish
before dark. The only luggage allowed in the Motive Power Depot will be cameras,
and photographs may be taken for private collection only.

     This permission is granted subject to the condition that the British Transport
Commission will not be responsible for the death or injury of any person exercising
this permission whilst on the Commission's premises, nor for any loss or damage to
the property of any such person however such death, injury, loss or damage may be
caused, and whether or not by the act, neglect or default of the Commission, their
servants or agents.

                                   Yours faithfully,
                                        FOR G. A. WEEDEN
                                        MOTIVE POWER OFFICER

Motive Power Depot to be visited	Date	Time	No. of Persons
NINE ELMS	MONDAY 31.8.59.	BETWEEN 9.0am/5.0pm	TWELVE 12

Master D.G.Copus,
1, Fernhurst Road,
SOUTHSEA.

THE PORTSMOUTH AREA DURING 1959

EVENING NEWS, MONDAY, MARCH 9, 1959—3

Rail Enthusiasts Tour Disused Branch Lines

FOR a few seconds, disused branch lines in Hampshire and Sussex sprang to life on Saturday afternoon as a train chartered from British Railways took members of the Branch Line Society over the rusting rails.

Some of the 130 people aboard came from Manchester for the trip, which lasted six hours.

A steam engine, towing two old-type carriages, left Portsmouth Harbour Station at 12.33 p.m., reaching Fishbourne Crossing 30 minutes later.

There the train reversed north to Lavant. The passenger service on the line, which used to go as far as Midhurst, was withdrawn in 1935, though a freight service has survived which now goes only to Lavant.

RETRACED PATH

From Lavant the train went to Chichester for water and then retraced its path via Farlington Halt and Cosham to Fareham.

After a short stop at Fareham the train went through Knowle Junction and Botley to Bishop's Waltham—closed to passenger traffic in 1933.

The train returned to Fareham for water and then went again to Knowle Junction, where it turned off for the Meon Valley line.

The complete Meon Valley line was from Alton to Fareham, and was one of the most picturesque in Hampshire. It has historical Associations with World War II for apart from its importance as a strategic alternative route to Portsmouth it was used for Sir Winston Churchill's train while it was a secret operation centre for military manoeuvres.

The Branch Line Society train went as far as Droxford, the actual place used by Sir Winston, and after a short halt returned through Fareham and on to Gosport, passing through Fort Brockhurst station.

The main line continues to Gosport Station which, once an architecturally impressive station, is now only a ruin. The station was originally built with two platforms and a centre siding enclosed by an overall roof and ornate buildings, as in the days of Queen Victoria who used the station when going to the Isle of Wight.

The train returned through Fareham to Portsmout' arriving at 6.30 p.m. after travelling over some of Hampshire's oldest lines and through its prettiest country.

FRATTON: SUNDAY 15 MARCH

This visit, in the company of David Copus, was made in the early evening. As we entered the shed gate a large coach party of railway enthusiasts from the Wolverhampton area arrived for a visit; we found out from one of the party that they were on a large-scale tour of locomotive depots in the south of England. We then visited the depot with the party and chatted to some of them, giving them information on engines allocated to Fratton - they seemed to be quite interested.

Left A news item of local interest, courtesy of *The News*, Portsmouth, formerly *Evening News*.

SOUTHSEA MINIATURE RAILWAY

Situated adjacent to Southsea beach, Southsea Miniature Railway proved to be a very big attraction during the summer months - I had many a ride in the late 1950s. It was a 10¼-inch gauge three-quarter-mile long line. Engine No 1003 *Victory*, seen in the accompanying newspaper photo, was a 4-4-2 and very popular with all ages. It was painted green with linings of brass and had a red background to its brass nameplates. Details: weight 1 ton 19 cwt; driving wheel diameter: 14 in; built by Southern Miniature Railways (but not the boiler); valve gear: Walschaerts. No 1002 *Valiant* was the engine formerly used.

Left **Mr Louis Hathaway with helper Roger Thomas prepares Southsea's miniature railway engine for the Easter weekend, 1959.** *Courtesy of The News, Portsmouth, formerly Evening News*

WESTERN REGION 4-6-0s AT FRATTON, 1959

A tremendous influx of Western Region named 4-6-0s, the majority of which were employed on excursions, were noted in Portsmouth during the summer months; those that I recorded are shown below. Class '4300' 2-6-0s also appeared at frequent intervals.

4901 *Adderley Hall*	6978 *Haroldstone Hall*	7801 *Anthony Manor*	7912 *Little Linford Hall*
4903 *Astley Hall*	6980 *Llanrumney Hall*	7900 *St Peter's Hall*	7920 *Coney Hall*
4918 *Dartington Hall*	6987 *Shervington Hall*	7907 *Hart Hall*	
4929 *Goytrey Hall*	6989 *Wightwick Hall*	7908 *Henshall Hall*	* In black livery
4932 *Hatherton Hall*	6996 *Blackwell Hall*	7910 *Hown Hall*	
4941 *Llangedwyn Hall*			
4942 *Maindy Hall*			
4954 *Plaish Hall*			
4967 *Shirenewton Hall*			
4969 *Shugborough Hall*			
4977 *Watcombe Hall*			
4989 *Cherwell Hall*			
4993 *Dalton Hall*			
4995 *Easton Hall*			
4998 *Eyton Hall*			
5903 *Keele Hall*			
5912 *Queen's Hall*			
5927 *Guild Hall*			
5931 *Hatherley Hall*			
5932 *Haydon Hall*			
5936 *Oakley Hall*			
5942 *Doldowlod Hall*			
5943 *Elmdon Hall*			
5947 *Saint Benet's Hall*			
5951 *Clyffe Hall*			
5956 *Horsley Hall*			
5966 *Ashford Hall*			
5977 *Beckford Hall*			
5982 *Harrington Hall*			
5994 *Roydon Hall*			
5995 *Wick Hall*			
5996 *Mytton Hall*			
6819 *Highnam Grange*			
6821 *Leaton Grange*			
6833 *Calcot Grange*			
6836 *Estevarney Grange*			
6848 *Toddington Grange*			
6853 *Morehampton Grange*			
6854 *Roundhill Grange*			
6857 *Tudor Grange*			
6872 *Crawley Grange*			
6907 *Davenham Hall*			
6908 *Downham Hall*			
6910 *Gossington Hall*			
6915 *Mursley Hall*			
6917 *Oldlands Hall*			
6924 *Grantley Hall**			
6934 *Beachamwell Hall*			
6942 *Eshton Hall*			
6948 *Holbrooke Hall*			
6949 *Haberfield Hall*			
6952 *Kimberley Hall*			
6961 *Stedham Hall*			
6967 *Willesley Hall*			
6975 *Capesthorne Hall*			
6977 *Grundisburgh Hall*			

Top The Monday-Saturday Reading to Portsmouth train makes a brisk re-start from platform 2 of Fratton station on the final stage of its journey, hauled by one of the Reading (81D)-allocated Class '4900' locomotives, No 5993 *Kirby Hall*.

Above 'Modified Hall' No 7920 *Coney Hall* takes a rest at the entrance to the depot round-house after bringing an excursion to Portsmouth Harbour from Gloucester on Sunday 2 August 1959. A further three 'Halls' were on shed on this day: Nos 5936 *Oakley Hall*, 6967 *Willesley Hall* and 7910 *Hown Hall*, all having brought excursions to Portsmouth Harbour. On the right (stored) is Class 'L1' 4-4-0 No 31757, an exile from Kent, due to electrification. Arriving in June 1959, it remained for almost a year before being towed away for scrapping.

FRATTON DEPOT

Steam locomotives:
30039 30349 30357 30544
30732 30850 31638 32337
32349 32479 32495 32509
32548 32549 32550 32640
32646 32650 32661 32677
32678 32694 34055 73114
76019

Diesel locomotive:
D3010

26 locomotives on shed (19 being Fratton allocations)

As on my previous visit, 0-6-0 tank locomotive No 30349 (Class 'G6') was once again noted. It was known to have been on loan from Guildford, which was obviously becoming a permanent loan. A named main-line locomotive, 'Lord Nelson' 4-6-0 No 30850

Lord Nelson, was an unusual visitor to this depot. Only one Class 'U' 2-6-0, No 31638, was on shed, but all three Class 'C2X' 0-6-0s were noted, these being Nos 32548, 32549 and 32550.

An excellent sight was the six Class 'A1X' 0-6-0 tanks, the motive power used on the Havant-Hayling Island branch. At the date of this visit these tanks had been re-allocated from Fratton to Eastleigh, and could be noted travelling in pairs (bunker to bunker) from Fratton depot to Havant. The six on shed were Nos 32640, 32646, 32650, 32661, 32677 and 32678.

The sole remaining Class 'E1' 0-6-0 tank locomotive, No 32694, introduced in 1874, was once again noted. In previous visits No 32139 had also been noted, but this had since been withdrawn and scrapped, so No 32694 was the one remaining 'E1' at Fratton depot. As mentioned in previous visits, its job was the daily goods train from Fratton to the Dockyard. Its route meant 'wrong line' working

through Portsmouth & Southsea (High Level) station to enable it to get on to the single line leading to the dockyard.

THE FRATTON SCENE: SUMMER OF 1959

Top right Class 'L1' 4-4-0 locomotive No 31757. Its chimney was at first covered with a tarpaulin, a sign of possible further use - but it was not to be, and the engine was eventually scrapped. Introduced in 1926, it probably spent all its working life in the Kent area employed on secondary passenger trains before being made redundant due to the Kent electrification scheme. This, in common with several other engines surplus to working requirements, was in store. Another little-known example of this practice at this time were the few steam engines stored away from the public eye in Brighton Works.

Top far right A close-up of the cab of No 31757. Shafts of sunlight reflect on the side window and cab as the locomotive awaits the ultimate call to the scrapyard.

Below left There was always a Class 'U' 2-6-0 locomotive to be seen at Fratton - No 31797 of Guildford is seen passing Fratton West signal box, on its way to the depot. Once again, the covered footbridge spanning the station platforms is prominent.

Right A varied selection of steam locomotives in the depot yard. On the left is Fratton-allocated Class 'M7' 0-4-4 tank No 30039, in the centre is 'Battle of Britain' 4-6-2 No 34059 *Sir Archibald Sinclair*, and on the right, letting off steam, is Class 'N' 2-6-0 No 31411.

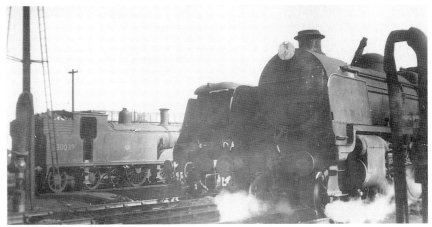

Centre right Standard Class '5' 4-6-0 passenger locomotive No 73089 *Maid of Astolat* near the depot entrance. Twenty of the total of 170 of this Class (introduced in 1951) were allocated to the Southern Region, and were used as replacement power for the 'King Arthurs' (Class 'N15') which were being withdrawn in the mid and late 1950s. The 20 locomotives acquired the following nameplates from the withdrawn 'N15s': *Merlin, Excalibur, Camelot, Pendragon, Tintagel, Melisande, The Green Knight, Linette, Joyous Gard, Maid of Astolat, The Red Knight, King Uther, Morgan le Fay, Lyonnesse, Etarre, King Pellinore, Iseult, Vivien, King Leodegrance* and finally *Elaine*. Numbers allocated were 73080 to 73089 and 73110 to 73119.

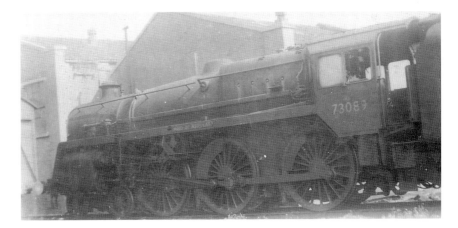

Bottom right Taking a quiet rest in a siding in the depot yard is Guildford-allocated Class 'U' 2-6-0 locomotive No 31799. There were 50 locomotives in this class, and they were very common in the Portsmouth area, often hauling secondary passenger trains on the Southampton, Eastleigh and Salisbury routes. No 31799 appears to be well coaled-up ready for its next duty.

SUMMER TIMETABLE 1959: NOTINGS OF INTEREST AT FRATTON

Eastern Region Class 'B1' 4-6-0 No 61119 (30A) arrived with an excursion from Leyton to Portsmouth Harbour on Wednesday 6 May.

Fratton-allocated Class 'M7' 0-4-4 tank No 30039 was seen entering platform 2 at Fratton with an 11-carriage Cardiff-Portsmouth train on Saturday 20 June! It had deputised for a failed engine, probably taking over at Fareham.

Class 'D1' 4-4-0 No 31735 (an exile from the Eastern Section) hauled the 12.15 pm Portsmouth & Southsea (Low Level) train to Plymouth as far as Fareham on 9 July and 8 August; on the latter date 'West Country' No 34098 *Templecombe* took over this train at Fareham.

WINTER 1959: NOTINGS OF INTEREST AT FRATTON

'Hall' Class 4-6-0s noted included No 4961 *Pyrland Hall* (10 October), No 4987 *Brockley Hall* (17 October) and No 5956 *Horsley Hall* (31 October).

Saturday 17 October saw 'West Country' No 34024 *Tamar Valley* come in with a football excursion from Plymouth (Portsmouth v Argyle).

Saturday 7 November saw Class 'L1' 4-4-0 No 31786 come in light, then out the same day.

Class 'Q1' 0-6-0 No 33020 (71A) brought in a four-carriage passenger train on the evening of 14 November.

On Sunday 13 December a double-headed excursion arrived at Portsmouth Harbour behind Nos 5926 *Grotrian Hall* and 4921 *Eaton Hall*.

Christmas parcels workings saw 'E1' 0-6-0 tank No 32694 (70F) employed ex-Gosport branch to Portsmouth with two vans. Class 'E4s' noted were Nos 32512 (75A) and 32509 (70F), on parcels.

Finally, 'Schools' No 30918 *Hurstpierpoint* arrived light on 19 December.

FRATTON: BOXING DAY, SATURDAY 26 DECEMBER

FRATTON DEPOT

Steam locomotives:
30349   30542   30544   30911
31628   31757   31807   32345
32636   32661   32678   32694
73117

Diesel locomotives:
D3013   D3040   D3665   D3666
15231

18 on shed, plus two Standard Class '4' 2-6-0s (numbers not known)

INDEX OF LOCATIONS

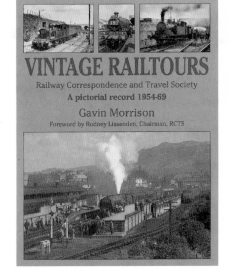